God's Battle

Making HIM Known

God's Battle
God's Names
God's Promise
God's Providence
God's Wisdom

God's Battle

BY SALLY MICHAEL

P U B L I S H I N G
P.O. BOX 817 • PHILLIPSBURG • NEW JERSEY 08865-0817

Unless otherwise indicated, Scripture quotations are from *ESV Bible* ® (*The Holy Bible, English Standard Version* ®). Copyright © 2001 by Crossway Bibles, a publishing ministry of Good News Publishers. Used by permission. All rights reserved.

Scripture quotations marked (NIV) are from the HOLY BIBLE, NEW INTERNATIONAL VERSION®. NIV®. Copyright © 1973, 1978, 1984 by International Bible Society. Used by permission of Zondervan Publishing House. All rights reserved.

ISBN: 978-1-59638-865-9 (pbk)
ISBN: 978-1-59638-866-6 (ePub)
ISBN: 978-1-59638-867-3 (Mobi)

Page design and typesetting by Dawn Premako

Printed in the United States of America

Library of Congress Control Number: 2014949379

Dedicated to
Kathi Westlund,
beloved friend, true sister,
and faithful prayer warrior.

May you continue to fight the fight of faith
as you labor in prayer for those you love
and for God's kingdom purposes.

Galatians 6:9

I have fought the good fight, I have finished the race, I have kept the faith. Henceforth there is laid up for me the crown of righteousness, which the Lord, the righteous judge, will award to me on that Day, and not only to me but also to all who have loved his appearing.
—2 Timothy 4:7–8

Contents

Preface 9

Introduction: How to Use This Book 12

1. Our Hearts 16

2. Our Actions Come from Our Hearts 20

3. Saved by Grace 24

4. Made Right Before God 28

5. The Battle Isn't Over 32

6. Be a Fighter! 36

7. The Battleground of Unbelief 40

8. The Battleground of Pride 44

9. The Battleground of Rebellion 48

10. The Battleground of Fear 52

11. The Battleground of Self 56

12. Never Give Up! 60

13. The Enemy's Attacks and Spiritual Weapons 64

14. More of the Enemy's Attacks 68

15. Even More of the Enemy's Attacks 72

16. Battle Strategy: Depend on God 76

17. Battle Strategy: Stand Guard 80

18. Battle Strategy: Be Prepared 84

19. Battle Strategy: Resist the Enemy 88

20. Battle Strategy: Renew Your Mind 92

21. Battle Strategy: Dwell on the Truth 96

22. Battle Strategy: Do Not Compromise 100

23. Battle Strategy: Confession 104

24. Battle Strategy: Demolish Strongholds............................. 108

25. Victory in Jesus!... 112

26. Aliens and Strangers 116

A Final Thought: Just Keep Stepping...................................120

Scripture Memory 121

Preface

Finally, be strong in the Lord
and in the strength of his might.
—Ephesians 6:10

Everyone is in a battle. Either you are fighting against God as an unbeliever, or you are a believer and God is helping you fight the fight of faith. Joining the fight of faith is a work of grace. Completing the fight of faith is also a work of grace, for it is God Himself who works in us so that we persevere in faith.

> And I am sure of this, that he who began a good work in you will bring it to completion at the day of Jesus Christ. (Philippians 1:6)

God's Battle is about persevering to the end. To persevere, one must fight. In a battle there is no room for passivity. There is no room for compromise. There is no vacation from the battle. You must fight . . . and you must keep on fighting. And you must never give up, because in Jesus there is the wonderful promise of victory and an eternal home.

If you are not fighting the battle of faith, you may not be a child of God. May God in His mercy save your soul. If you are fighting the battle, God has given you ample weapons to fight the good fight, and He is working in you. Do not be afraid of the enemy; do not grow weary in the battle; do not despair of the fight . . .

> for he who is in you is greater than he who is in the world. (1 John 4:4)

We are not alone in the fight of faith. God Himself fights with us to keep us persevering in faith until the end. And God is always victorious.

In the pages of this book there is a battle strategy to fight for your faith. May you, the parent, fight well, and in turn encourage your child to fight well. May you finish your race well and fight the good fight to the end. May we all trust in Jesus to the end and say when we see Him face to face,

I have fought the good fight, I have finished the race, I have kept the faith. (2 Timothy 4:7)

A mighty fortress is our God, a bulwark never failing;
Our helper He amid the flood of mortal ills prevailing.
For still our ancient foe doth seek to work us woe;
His craft and power are great; and, armed with cruel hate,
On earth is not his equal.

Did we in our own strength confide, our striving would be losing;
Were not the right Man on our side, the Man of God's own choosing.
Dost ask who that may be? Christ Jesus, it is He;
Lord Sabaoth His Name, from age to age the same,
And He must win the battle.

And though this world, with devils filled, should threaten to undo us,
We will not fear, for God hath willed His truth to triumph through us.
The Prince of Darkness grim, we tremble not for him;
His rage we can endure, for lo! his doom is sure;
One little word shall fell him.

That word above all earthly powers, no thanks to them, abideth;
The Spirit and the gifts are ours through Him Who with us sideth;
Let goods and kindred go, this mortal life also;
The body they may kill: God's truth abideth still;
 His kingdom is forever.

—"A Mighty Fortress Is Our God," Martin Luther, 1529;
   trans. Frederick H. Hedge, 1853

Introduction
How to Use This Book

This book was written to give parents an opportunity to present solid truth to their children and to encourage real-life application of that truth.

Relational

Children receive more encouragement to learn when truth is presented by a trusted individual. Your positive, relational parent-child commitment will be a real benefit when you sit down together to read this book. Your time together over the Word should be positive, affirming, and loving.

Interactive

There is a greater impact when an individual *discovers* truth instead of just hearing it presented. Many questions have been incorporated into the text of this book to encourage your child to wonder and think critically. The process of discovery will be circumvented if you don't give your child adequate time to think and respond. After asking a question, wait for a response. If your child has difficulty, ask the question in a different way or give a few hints.

Questions and responses can be springboards for more questions and discovery as you interact with your child's mind and heart. The Holy Spirit is the real teacher, so depend on Him to give both you and your child thoughts and truths to explore together, and to bring the necessary understanding. Take the time to work through each story at a leisurely pace—giving time for interaction and further dialogue. The goal should be to get the material into the child, not just to get the child through the material.

Understandable

These stories have been written with attention given to explaining difficult or potentially new concepts. Some of these concepts may take time for your child to digest. Allow your child to ponder new truths. Read the story more than once, allowing the truth to be better understood and integrated into your child's theological framework. At times, have your child read parts of the lesson, giving an opportunity for visual learning.

Because vocabulary can be child-specific, define the particular words foreign to your child. Retell difficult sections in familiar wording, and ask questions to be sure your child understands the truth being taught.

Theological

More than just acquainting your child with an understanding of spiritual warfare, this book is building a foundation of biblical theology for your child. As your child begins to correctly understand who God is, who Satan is, the spiritual battle every person is in, and the weapons of victory God gives His children, your child will begin to see the reality of the spiritual world and the beauty of God and His ways.

Because the Word of God has convicting and converting power, Bible texts are quoted word for word in some parts. Some of these verses may be beyond the child's understanding, so you may want to explain unfamiliar words or thoughts. Even though clear comprehension may be difficult, hearing the Word itself is a means that the Holy Spirit often uses to encourage faith in your child (Romans 10:17). Do not minimize the effectual influence of God's Word in the tender souls of children.

Since the Word of God is living and active, allow the child to read the actual Bible verses as much as possible. Also, encourage your child to memorize some of the verses so he or she can meditate on them at other times.

The gospel is presented numerous times throughout the book. Use this as an opportunity to share God's work of grace in your life, and to converse with your child about his or her spiritual condition. Be careful not to confuse spiritual interest with converting faith, and take care to avoid giving premature assurances. Fan the flames of gospel-inspired conviction and tenderness toward the sacrificial love of Jesus without prematurely encouraging your child to pray "the sinner's prayer."[1]

Application

Understanding the truth is essential, but understanding alone is insufficient. Truth must also be embraced in the heart and acted upon in daily life. Often, children cannot make the connection between a biblical truth and real-life application, so you, the parent, must help bridge the gap.

Consider the following quotation by D. Martyn Lloyd-Jones:

> We must always put things in the right order, and it is Truth first. . . . The heart is always to be influenced through the understanding—the mind, then the heart, then the will. . . . But God forbid that anyone should think that it ends with the intellect. It starts there, but it goes on. It then moves the heart and finally the man yields his will. He obeys, not grudgingly or unwillingly, but with the whole heart. The Christian life is a glorious perfect life that takes up and captivates the entire personality.[2]

Spend a few days or even a week on each story. Reread the story, discuss the truths, and follow the suggestions in the Learning to Trust God section. Most

1. Some excellent resources for parents regarding the salvation of children can be found at www.children desiringgod.org, including a booklet titled *Helping Children to Understand the Gospel* and two seminars from the 2007 Children Desiring God conference, How Great a Salvation—"Leading Children to a Solid Faith" and "Presenting the Gospel to Children."

2. D. Martyn Lloyd-Jones, *Spiritual Depression* (Grand Rapids: William B. Eerdmans, 1965), 61–62.

importantly, help your child to see that God is who He says He is, and help him or her to act in response to the truth. Point out God's involvement in daily life and thank Him for being true to His Word.

Prayer

Ultimately, our efforts are effective only if the Holy Spirit breathes on our teaching and quickens it to the heart. Pray not only before going through the stories, but also in the succeeding days, that your child would see the beauty of God and His ways and respond to Him in faith.

Our Hearts

Has your mother or father ever fixed something that was broken? What was it? People can fix a lot of things: flat tires, a shirt with a missing button, and lawn mowers. Sometimes doctors can even fix really important things, like a weak heart.

But there is a heart problem no doctor can ever fix—a very, very serious heart problem. It can't be fixed with medicine or an operation . . . and every single person except Jesus is born with this heart problem. That includes Abraham in the Bible, King David, Mary and Joseph, your grandparents, your parents . . . and you.

The heart with the problem is not the one that pumps blood through our bodies. But it is the heart the Bible talks about, which is your deepest thoughts and feelings and the things you love most. This is what the Bible says about the heart:

The Lord saw that the wickedness of man was great in the earth, and that every intention of the thoughts of his heart was only evil continually. (Genesis 6:5)

What words in this verse show you how bad the heart is? "Every," "only," "continually." Is the heart just a little bit bad or very seriously evil? It is very seriously evil, and this very serious heart problem makes us turn away from God. It keeps us from loving and doing what we should. It makes us love sin and struggle to do what is right. Our hearts don't naturally love being generous, or being more concerned about others than about ourselves, or being told we can't get our own way.

Do you know how our hearts got this way? They got this way the same way King David's heart got this way.

> Surely I was sinful at birth,
> sinful from the time my mother conceived me. (Psalm 51:5 NIV)

When David was born, and even before he was born, he had a sinful heart. And we did too. Every person is born with a sinful heart; we can't change that. Just like we can't change what color of eyes we have, how tall we will be, or what we will be good at, we can't change the kind of heart we have.

Some things become damaged—like new tennis shoes worn in the mud, or a torn shirt, or a rusty bike. But not our hearts. They came with a sin problem.

If something is dirty, you can wash it. If it is torn, you can sew it. If a screw is missing, you can put in a new screw. If something is dented, you can pound out the dent. But there is nothing we can do to fix our sinful hearts.

That is really BAD NEWS! It is bad news because God hates sin and cannot accept anyone with a sinful heart. This is what the Bible says about God:

> You who are of purer eyes than to see evil
> and cannot look at wrong . . . (Habakkuk 1:13)

There is no evil in God. He is pure—good and right. He cannot even stand to look at sin! With our sinful hearts, we cannot have a friendship with God. We have no right to enter heaven. Instead, we deserve eternal punishment in hell. This is *horrible* news for sinners who cannot fix their sinful hearts. This should make us all very sad, scared, and upset.

But there is more to the story. There is also GOOD NEWS! Very, very, very good news. It is good news that should make us full of joy, unafraid, and peaceful.

Do you want to know the good news? To know the good news, you need to keep reading this book. See if you can discover the very, very, very good news . . . the best news ever!

LEARNING TO TRUST GOD

✢ Read Genesis 6:5–8, 11–22. What is thes bad news in this Bible story? What shows you that there is good news?

✢ Read Romans 3:23. How have you sinned? What does it mean to "fall short of the glory of God"?

✢ *Activity:* Take a glass of milk and add some dirt to it. Would you drink it? Why not? Can you take the dirt out of the milk? How is the dirty milk like our hearts? How does this experiment help you to understand Habakkuk 1:13? Why can't God accept sinful man?

Our Actions Come from Our Hearts

When you cut an orange, what kind of smell comes out? Does an onion smell come out of an orange? No. Where does an onion smell come from? An onion. An orange smell comes from an orange, and an onion smell comes from an onion. What comes out is determined by what is inside.

It's the same way with our hearts. What comes out is determined by what is inside. This is what the Bible says about it:

> The good person out of the good treasure of his heart produces good, and the evil person out of his evil treasure produces evil, for out of the abundance of the heart his mouth speaks. (Luke 6:45)

Good things come from good hearts; bad things come from bad hearts. What we do and say comes from our hearts. Taking the biggest cookie, the best seat, or the most markers comes from what is in the heart. Taking the small cookie, or giving someone else the best seat, or sharing your markers also comes from what is in the heart.

See how you do on this quiz about the heart:

- What is in the heart that makes a person take the best for himself? (maybe selfishness or greed)
- What is in the heart when a person helps someone who falls down? (maybe kindness or compassion)
- When a person calls another person a name or hits someone else, what is in his heart? (maybe meanness or jealousy or anger)

Most often what we do and say comes from what is deep in our hearts. Sometimes we don't even realize what is in our hearts. But what is in our hearts affects what we say and do.

People with good hearts *most often* do and say good things. Even though sometimes people with good hearts do bad things, *most of the time* they do and say good things. People with bad hearts will do and say bad things. It is very hard for us not to follow what our hearts want.

Do you think a person can make himself do what is right when in his heart he wants to do what is wrong? Let's find out!

Think about a rubber band, or go get a rubber band if you have one. Can you stretch it out and make it longer? Yes, you can. By pulling on it and holding it tightly you can make it longer. But what happens when you let go? The rubber band goes back to being smaller. It goes back to what it most naturally is. For how long can you stretch the rubber band? Can you stretch it forever? No, at some point you let go of it.

Our hearts are the same way. We can make ourselves do good things we don't really want to do—it is like making the rubber band longer. We are pulling our hearts away from what is wrong to make them go the right way. But sooner or later, we get tired and give up. We let go.

When a person's heart is wrong, he can force himself to do what is right, but sooner or later he will snap back to do what his heart really wants to do. His heart keeps pulling him back to what is wrong. He just isn't strong enough to keep doing what is right.

It is not enough to try to *do* the right thing. That doesn't last. We have all been born with a sinful heart.

No one is good except God alone. (Mark 10:18)[1]

One of the things we need is a new heart, a heart that loves what is right. We need a heart that loves God and His ways and that *wants* to do and say good things. But how can we get a new heart? We can't buy it at the store or get it for Christmas. We can't make one or fix the one we have.

We are back to the BAD NEWS: our sinful hearts cannot be accepted by a holy God. Trying to do what is right does not make us have a good heart.

The Bible tells us about a man who thought he was good. He thought the good things he did would get him into heaven. We don't know his name; the Bible calls him the rich young ruler. He told Jesus that he kept all the commandments—did

---

1. If your child wonders why the Bible says that God alone is good and also talks about the good person in Luke 6:45, explain that Jesus can give people a *measure* of His goodness.

the right things. But Jesus knew about the man's heart. He knew that he didn't love God most of all, even though he was doing many good things. He loved his money and the things it could buy most of all.

So Jesus told him to sell everything he owned and give the money to poor people. Do you know what the man did? He went away very sad. He knew that he loved his money more than he loved God. He also knew that he could not change his heart.

This is the bad news for all of us. We cannot change our sinful hearts. So how could anyone be saved from a sinful heart and go to heaven?

With man this is impossible, but with God all things are possible. (Matthew 19:26)

LEARNING TO TRUST GOD

✦ Read Luke 6:43–45 and explain what it means. Where do our actions come from?

✦ Read the story of the rich young ruler in Matthew 19:16–30. What did Jesus ask the young man to give up? What do those who follow Jesus receive? Which is the greater treasure? Pray that Jesus will be the greatest treasure in your heart.

✦ *Activity:* Put a few teaspoons of baking soda into a small container. Then add vinegar. What happens? How is the way that the mixture bubbles up and fizzes over like the actions of our hearts?

Saved by Grace

Do you remember the very bad and horrible news? Everyone is born with a sinful heart that keeps us from loving God and what is good and right. Our hearts are stubborn, and we don't want to follow God. From the day we are born we are fighting against God. So we deserve God's anger and punishment.

> But because of your hard and impenitent heart you are storing up wrath for yourself on the day of wrath when God's righteous judgment will be revealed. (Romans 2:5)

Just like squirrels store up acorns for winter, we sin and store up God's anger or wrath. On the day of judgment, God will send unrepentant sinners—those who are fighting against Him—to hell. That is very bad news for sinners born with sinful hearts.

But remember that there is very, very, very wonderful GOOD NEWS too! Do you know what it is?

> For by grace you have been saved through faith. And this is not your own doing; it is the gift of God. (Ephesians 2:8)

The good news is *grace*. Grace is God's kindness to undeserving sinners. We do not deserve any favor from God. But God is kind to give sinners the gift of *faith*. A gift is not something you earn or deserve. It is given to you because the person who gives the gift is kind and loving.

Do you know what faith is? Suppose you are standing on something high. Your grandpa tells you to jump and he will catch you. Having faith in your grandpa means you can trust him. He will do what he says—he will catch you. You know that he is kind and does not lie, so you can believe what he says. He won't turn away or ignore you. You can depend on him to catch you.

Faith in God is trusting and depending on God. It is believing what He promises and believing that God is who He says He is. It is trusting Him to solve your sin problem through His grace. It is saying, "Jesus, I want you." It is trusting that Jesus took the punishment for your sins on the cross. When God puts faith in a person's heart to trust Jesus to forgive his sins, that person is saved from the wrath and punishment of God.

That is the greatest news! You can be forgiven of your sins and saved from the wrath of God! But how does this happen? You can't change your heart to want to trust God.

Remember that faith is a *gift*. This is what God does:

And I will give you a new heart, and a new spirit I will put within you. And I will remove the heart of stone from your flesh and give you a heart of flesh. (Ezekiel 36:26)

You can't change your heart . . . but God can give you a *new* heart! You were born with a stubborn, sinful heart that does not want God—a hard heart, a "heart of stone." But God can give you a new "heart of flesh"—a soft heart that is not rebellious, a heart that wants God, a heart of faith.

Then you aren't fighting against God anymore! It is like when you are wrestling with your dad. He is stronger than you and can hold you down so you can't move. When you stop struggling, what do you say? You say, "I give up."

In the same way, the new heart of flesh says, "I give up. I give up doing things my way. I give up trying to be good enough to get to heaven on my own. I give up depending on myself." The heart of flesh stops fighting against God. Instead, the person with a new heart joins the "fight of faith"—the fight to keep trusting in God. He is now a child of God with a special friendship with God. This is the best gift of all and the greatest good news!

The big question is, what kind of heart do you have—a heart of stone or a heart of flesh? Are you fighting against God, wanting to go your own way, or are you fighting the fight of faith?

Take a quick look at the cover of this book. What did you notice? What color is the title? What did you see in the picture? Now *examine* the cover—look at it very closely. Take your time and think about each part. Did you notice new things? When we examine things—look at them very closely and thoughtfully—we see things we didn't see before.

This is what Paul tells us to do about our hearts:

Examine yourselves, to see whether you are in the faith. Test yourselves. Or do you not realize this about yourselves, that Jesus Christ is in you?—unless indeed you fail to meet the test! (2 Corinthians 13:5)

What do you test? You test your heart. What do you truly love most? Do you love the Word of God? Do you love generosity, kindness, and patience? What attitudes do you have? Do you hate sin? Examine your heart and remember the very bad news and the very good news.

LEARNING TO TRUST GOD

✳ Read Romans 2:5 again. What do the words "impenitent," "wrath," "day of wrath," "righteous," "judgment," and "revealed" mean? Now explain the verse to someone else in your own words.

✳ Read Romans 5:12, 15–16. What do we get from Adam? What does Jesus give sinners?

✳ *Activity:* Look at something (a bug, a flower, a tree) and see what you notice. Then examine it very closely. Now what do you notice about it? Talk about how to examine your heart. What questions should you ask yourself? What should you notice about your heart this week?

Made Right Before God

Do you know what a driver's license is? It is a card from the government saying that a person can drive a car. A marriage license is a paper from the government saying that a man and a woman are married—they are husband and wife. The law says that for two people to be married, they must have a marriage license. If they don't have one, they aren't married.

But even though being married started with a marriage license, the relationship—the friendship—of the man and woman did not start with a marriage license. Two strangers didn't decide to get married. Something happened first in the heart of the man and the woman. What was it?

It was love. Love grew in the man's heart for the woman and in the woman's heart for the man. Then they decided to get married and got a marriage license. After their wedding, the law says they are husband and wife.

It works the same way in salvation. First the heart is changed from fighting against God to trusting in Him. It is impossible for a person to change his heart. But God can change a stubborn, sinful heart. He gives a person a gift—a new heart and the faith to trust in Him.

Before God changes a person's heart, the person is far from God. He has broken God's good laws. He is guilty of not keeping God's laws. *Guilty* means he disobeyed the law. The law of God says that this person is a law-breaker, not a law-keeper. He is not right; he is *unright*eous. He is a sinner who deserves punishment from God.

Mary was a sinner. She was not a good person; instead, she had broken God's law many times. She was guilty and deserved punishment. But Jesus makes bad hearts new and right.

Mary heard that Jesus was invited to eat at the house of a man named Simon. So she took a bottle of very precious ointment—a strong, nice-smelling perfume—and went to see Jesus.

And standing behind him at his feet, weeping, she began to wet his feet with her tears and wiped them with the hair of her head and kissed his feet and anointed them with the ointment. (Luke 7:38)

How much do you think Mary loved Jesus?

Simon thought he was a good man. He thought he was a law-keeper and not a sinner like Mary. When he saw what Mary was doing, he was upset and disgusted. He could not believe Jesus would let a woman like Mary touch him.

Jesus knew what Simon was thinking. He also knew what was in Mary's and Simon's hearts.

Then turning toward the woman he said to Simon, "Do you see this woman? I entered your house; you gave me no water for my feet, but she has wet my feet with her tears and wiped them with her hair. You gave me no kiss,

but from the time I came in she has not ceased to kiss my feet. You did not anoint my head with oil, but she has anointed my feet with ointment. Therefore I tell you, her sins, which are many, are forgiven—for she loved much." (Luke 7:44–47)

Jesus knew Simon thought he was righteous—a good man, not a sinner. Jesus knew that Simon did not love Him. But Mary knew she was a sinner and deserved punishment. God had put faith and love in her heart. And Jesus forgave her sins and called her "not guilty." Jesus was a perfect law-keeper who gave Mary His perfect law-keeping.

When God changes a person's heart and gives him a heart of faith, God calls that person "not guilty" and declares him to be *right*eous. His sins are forgiven, and God does not punish him for his sins. Jesus, who never sinned and was always right, took the person's punishment on the cross. And the person also gets the righteousness of Jesus given to him.

This is like math. When God calls a person "righteous," two things happen. There is a subtraction and an addition. The person's guilt is subtracted—the punishment for sin is taken away. And Jesus' perfect law-keeping—His righteousness—is added.

- guilt and punishment
+ perfect law-keeping (righteousness)

There is another way to understand what Jesus did on the cross for sinners. It is like taking a test and having all the wrong answers. Jesus erases all the wrong answers. But Jesus does more than that! He puts His right answers in their place. The wrong answers are like our sin. When we trust in Jesus, He erases sin and also gives us His perfect law-keeping. Jesus makes sinners righteous before God.

Is this GOOD NEWS? It was good news for Mary. And it can be good news for you. Instead of looking at you and seeing *sin*, God can look at you and see the *cross*, which takes away your sin and gives you Jesus' righteousness. Do you have faith in Jesus? Do you love what He did on the cross?

There is therefore now no condemnation for those who are in Christ Jesus. (Romans 8:1)

LEARNING TO TRUST GOD

✤ Read the story of Mary's love for Jesus and Jesus' forgiveness in Luke 7:36–50. What does this story tell you about Jesus? About forgiveness? Ask Jesus to give you a heart of faith.

✤ Read Romans 8:1. What does "condemnation" mean? What does "in Christ Jesus" mean?

✤ *Activity:* What can your family do out of love for Jesus? (Hint: read Matthew 25:34–40.) Come up with an idea and do it.

The Battle Isn't Over

S uppose a person plays the violin and is chosen to be in an orchestra or music group. Would he say, "Hurray! Now that I am in the orchestra, I don't have to practice anymore!"? Why not? Being in the orchestra means he needs to practice more! He needs to learn new music and go to the practices so he can play well in concerts.

Just as the work of practicing and playing the violin doesn't end when a person joins the orchestra, so the work of fighting sin and fighting for faith doesn't end when a person becomes a Christian. He can't say, "Well, now everything will be easy. I can just relax. I don't need to read my Bible or pray, because I am saved. Satan will leave me alone now. I have a new heart, so I don't have to fight against sin or grow in faith."

Even with a new heart, a "heart of flesh," the old sin nature that loves what is wrong is still in the heart. The old nature wasn't subtracted, but a new nature was added:

old sin nature (weakened) + new heart and new nature

The old sin nature fights against the new heart that loves God and what is good and right. So every Christian is in a fight or a battle. Before, he was in a fight against God. Now he is fighting for his faith and against sin with the help of God.

Satan tries to make Christians stop trusting God. He tries to make them turn against God and think that the Bible isn't true. Every Christian has to fight *against* Satan and fight *for* his faith. He fights to trust God in all things, to read the Bible, and to love the truth of God's Word. He must fight against sin and battle to do good and to say what is kind. This is a serious battle.

Paul calls this battle "working out your salvation."

Work out your own salvation with fear and trembling, for it is God who works in you, both to will and to work for his good pleasure. (Philippians 2:12–13)

The fight against sin and the fight for faith doesn't end. Christians need to fight the fight of faith all their lives. But we don't have to fight alone! God, the almighty Ruler of the Universe, helps us. God makes us strong and puts love for Him and what is good in our hearts. God brings other Christians to help us fight the fight of faith. And God gives us His Word as a mighty sword.

There is a story in the Bible that will help you to understand this. It is the story of a long, fierce battle and how God helped His people when they were in the wilderness. The people of Amalek came to fight the people of Israel.

> So Moses said to Joshua, "Choose for us men, and go out and fight with Amalek. Tomorrow I will stand on the top of the hill with the staff of God in my hand." So Joshua did as Moses told him, and fought with Amalek, while Moses, Aaron, and Hur went up to the top of the hill. (Exodus 17:9–10)

Why did Moses hold up his staff? He was asking for God's help. When Moses held up his staff, Israel was winning the battle. God was helping them. They weren't fighting alone.

But what do you think happened after a while? Moses' arms got tired. The battle was long, and Moses couldn't keep holding up his arms to ask for God's help. How long can you hold up your arms? Try and see how long you can hold them up while you read the rest of this story.

When Moses put his tired arms down, the people of Amalek were winning . . . and Israel was losing the battle. Israel needed God's help. They could not win the battle alone.

> But Moses' hands grew weary, so they took a stone and put it under him, and he sat on it, while Aaron and Hur held up his hands, one on one side, and the other on the other side. So his hands were steady until the going down of the sun. (Exodus 17:12)

When Moses' arms got tired, Aaron and Hur helped him hold up his arms. Israel needed help from God to fight the battle, and Moses needed help from Aaron and Hur to hold up his arms in prayer. With God's help, Joshua and his army won the battle. With God fighting for Israel, their enemy could not defeat them.

God fights for His people. He does not leave us alone in our battles. He helps us to fight the fight of faith. He does not just help us for a little while and then decide He is tired of helping us. He keeps helping His people. He starts the work of faith in the hearts of His children, and someday He will finish that work and bring His children home to heaven.

And I am sure of this, that he who began a good work in you will bring it to completion at the day of Jesus Christ. (Philippians 1:6)

Are your arms tired yet? Are you still holding them up? God never gets tired. If you are His child, He will help you fight to grow strong in faith.

LEARNING TO TRUST GOD

✦ Read Philippians 2:12–13. What does "work out your own salvation" mean? Why does Paul say "with fear and trembling"? What does this verse say about a Christian's effort and God's grace? Are you fighting against God, or is God helping you to fight the fight of faith? Ask God to show you the condition of your heart.

✦ Read about the battle between Israel and Amalek in Exodus 17:8–16. What can you learn about fighting the fight of faith from this story? What did God want to teach his people in this story?

✦ *Activity:* Like Aaron and Hur, we can help those who are weary in the battle. How can your family help a Christian friend to fight the fight of faith? Do something to encourage a weary Christian.

Be a Fighter!

Do you know that there are invisible things in this world? There are! You can't see the air you breathe or the smells you smell. But they are real. You can't see a sound wave, but you can hear talking, whistles, and music. What about gravity that holds you on the ground? You can't see any of these things. They are invisible to us.

Did you know that there is also an invisible battle? You are part of it. You can't see it with your eyes, because it is not a battle fought with fists or muscles. It isn't fought with swords or bombs either. It is not a physical battle. It is a spiritual battle—the battle of faith. This is what the Bible says about it:

Finally, be strong in the Lord and in the strength of his might. Put on the whole armor of God, that you may be able to stand against the schemes of the devil. For we do not wrestle against flesh and blood, but against the rulers, against the authorities, against the cosmic powers over this present darkness, against the spiritual forces of evil in the heavenly places. Therefore take up the whole armor of God, that you may be able to withstand in the evil day, and having done all, to stand firm. (Ephesians 6:10–13)

What does the Bible say we are supposed to do in this battle? It says to be strong in the Lord, put on God's armor, wrestle, and stand firm. We are to fight! This is a battle, and in a battle you fight to win. You can't "sort of" fight or just watch the battle. You can't run away or give up. You have to get in there and fight with all your might!

If you are a Christian, God fights this battle with you. Does that mean you can just take it easy, sit back, and rest? No, even though God is strong, He asks us to fight. If you want to be a strong Christian, you must be a strong fighter. You will have to fight against your sin nature and fight for greater faith in God.

Suppose your mother leaves two treats, one big and one little—one for you and one for your brother. Your brother thinks *he* should get the big treat, and you think *you* should get the big treat. So you start to argue and fight with each other.

What is the real battle? Is it between you and your brother? No, the real fight is not against "flesh and blood"—you against your brother. The fight is against selfishness. But even more than that, the real battle is a fight of faith. Will you trust that God's ways are best and that God's Word is true when it says that "it is more blessed to give than to receive" (Acts 20:35)?

When God told Moses that He would free His people from slavery in Egypt, He also promised that He would give them the land of Canaan—"a good and broad land, a land flowing with milk and honey" (Exodus 3:8). Before taking the land of Canaan, Moses sent twelve spies to check out the land. When they came back, the spies said it was a very good land—just like God said. But the people of Canaan were strong and had well-protected cities.

Ten of the spies said,

> We are not able to go up against the people, for they are stronger than we are. (Numbers 13:31)

But Joshua and Caleb told the people that they could take the land, even though they knew the people were big and strong. This is what Joshua said:

> If the LORD delights in us, he will bring us into this land and give it to us, a land that flows with milk and honey. Only do not rebel against the LORD. . . . The LORD is with us; do not fear them. (Numbers 14:8–9)

The people of Israel did not believe Joshua and Caleb.

What was the real battle? Was it Joshua and Caleb fighting against the other spies and the people? The real battle was a battle against fear. It was a battle to believe God's promise. It was a battle to trust God to give them the land. It was a spiritual battle—a battle of faith.

When David faced the giant Goliath, he wasn't *just* fighting against Goliath. He was fighting a spiritual battle. "Do I believe that God is greater than Goliath? Do I believe that God will help me? Do I believe that God will defend His people?" David won that battle. He trusted God, and God gave him perfect aim with his sling—and the giant Goliath fell down dead. More than that, God helped David to fight the fight of faith, and David trusted God.

All of life, everything you face, has an invisible spiritual side to it, and you face spiritual battles every day. Paul tells us what to do in those battles. Does he tell us to be afraid of the battle or to run away? No! Paul tells us to jump in and fight the battle! He tells us to put on God's armor and take our stand. Then we are to fight with everything in us and with God's help!

Fight the good fight of the faith. (1 Timothy 6:12)

LEARNING TO TRUST GOD

✤ Read the story of the twelve spies in Numbers 13:17–14:11, 26–30. What lies did the people of Israel believe? What truth did Joshua and Caleb believe? What was the consequence of not trusting God?

✤ What spiritual battles did you face this week? How did you fight them?

✤ *Activity:* Find some pictures of knights in armor. How do the different pieces of armor help to protect the knight? What pieces help him to fight against his enemy? Read Ephesians 6:10–18 and draw a picture of the Christian's armor.

The Battleground of Unbelief

Have you ever seen a "tug of war"? It is played with two teams and a rope. Each team holds an end of the rope. A line is drawn in the dirt with a team on each side of the line. When the tug of war starts, each team pulls on the rope. One team pulls one way, and the other team pulls the other way. The team that pulls the other team over the line wins.

There is something like a tug of war in our hearts. Even for Christians who are trusting in Jesus, there is a war between really trusting God and wondering whether God can be trusted. There is a battle between whether to trust God in all things or to depend on ourselves. There is a tug of war in the heart between *knowing* that we can trust God and actually *trusting* God.

This is the same tug of war that the Israelites had. God had done many wonders for them. He saved them from slavery in Egypt. He opened the Red Sea so they could walk through it. When they had no water in the wilderness, He split rocks and water poured out! God showed Israel that He is faithful and powerful and that they could trust Him.

But the Israelites still had a battle in their hearts between trusting in God and unbelief—not trusting that He really is a mighty, loving, wise God.

Yet they sinned still more against him,
    rebelling against the Most High in the desert.
They tested God in their heart
    by demanding the food they craved.
They spoke against God, saying,
    "Can God spread a table in the wilderness?
He struck the rock so that water gushed out
    and streams overflowed.

Can he also give bread
    or provide meat for his people?" (Psalm 78:17–20)

The Israelites doubted God. They wondered, "Can God give us bread and meat?" They weren't sure He could do it. They weren't sure that God would take care of them. Maybe they would starve. They looked at the emptiness of the desert and didn't believe that God could do anything He wanted.

How do you think God felt about that?

Therefore, when the Lord heard, he was full of wrath;
    . . . .
    his anger rose against Israel,

because they did not believe in God
    and did not trust his saving power. (Psalm 78:21–22)

Why was God angry? He was angry because His people did not trust Him. But still God was good to them. He rained down manna bread from the sky for them to eat. He even sent quail birds that flew right to their camp . . . and made them fall down for the Israelites to eat! God can be trusted! He is powerful and loving! He takes care of His children.

Even though the Israelites doubted God, He took care of them. They didn't believe that God would give them food. But He did. He is a faithful God who can be trusted. He proved to Israel that He is a mighty and good God. Surely Israel would now trust Him.

Do you think the Israelites would know now that they could trust God? No. They *still* had a battle in their hearts to trust God! But instead of fighting to trust God, they gave up. They let unbelief—not trusting and believing in God—win in their hearts.

In spite of all this, they still sinned;
    despite his wonders, they did not believe. (Psalm 78:32)

When we think about Israel, we wonder how they could be so wrong. How could they be so foolish as to doubt God? They had seen so many miracles!

But we are very much like Israel. God has proved Himself to be mighty, good, and wise. He has shown us that He can be trusted. The battle to believe or not to believe is often still in our hearts. When something bad happens, do we really believe that God knows about it and will help us? When we are afraid, do we really trust that God will take care of us? Although we want to trust God, sometimes unbelief creeps into our hearts. Our faith is sometimes very weak. And the battle to believe or not to believe is very strong.

Do you know that even great men of faith in the Bible sometimes battled against unbelief? Even Abraham, Moses, David, and Peter had to battle against unbelief. But God has given His children a mighty weapon to fight unbelief. This weapon is mentioned in the book of Psalms, which says,

> I will remember the deeds of the Lord;
>> yes, I will remember your wonders of old.
> I will ponder all your work,
>> and meditate on your mighty deeds. (Psalm 77:11–12)

What is the mighty weapon? Is it a sword or a club? Is it a pill that we take that helps our hearts to believe? No, the mighty weapon is *remembering*! Remembering the mighty ways God has worked for His people. Remembering that God opened the Red Sea, closed the mouths of lions to protect Daniel, and saved Noah in the ark. Remembering David's sling and the giant Goliath, bread and water in the wilderness, and Jesus quieting the storm. What other mighty deeds of God can you remember?

When your faith is weak, *remember*. Remember what God has done. Remember His wonders. Think about and remember the great things God has done, and fight to trust God.

LEARNING TO TRUST GOD

✦ Read Exodus 16:1–15. How did God show that He can be trusted?

✦ Ask your mother or father what mighty deeds God has done in their lives. How has this helped them to trust Him?

✦ *Activity:* As a family, make a booklet to remind you of the deeds of the Lord. You could include verses, pictures, or a retelling of the story. When you need to fight the battle to trust God, look through the booklet and remember the mighty deeds of God.

The Battleground of Pride

Have you ever heard it said that someone has a "big head'? What does that mean? Usually this is not about the size of a person's head. It usually means that the person is proud. He thinks he is really important and better than other people. He thinks he knows more than he does, and he doesn't like it when someone gives him advice. He thinks his way of doing things is best and the ideas of other people aren't worth listening to. It is hard for a person who is proud to admit when he is wrong or to say that he is sorry. That's because a proud person always wants to be right.

Not everyone is proud. What is the opposite of proud? It is humble. A proud person thinks he is very important when he does something well. But a humble person understands that everything he does well comes from God. Every good grade you get is because God gave you a smart brain or the desire to work really hard. Everyone who sings beautifully has a beautiful voice because God gave it to him. Any ability we have is a gracious, undeserved gift from God.

Do you do something really well? Maybe you can sing beautifully or play baseball really well. People may say, "You have a beautiful voice," or, "You are a great ball player!" How might a proud person respond? He might say, "Yes, I know," or, "I'll do even better next time."

What is a humble response? It might be a prayer praising God, such as, "God, my voice is a gift from You. This praise I got is for You." Or it might be saying to the person, "I prayed that God would help me and He did. God is so faithful." The humble person knows that "every good gift and every perfect gift" comes from God (James 1:17).

What happens when you blow into a balloon . . . and blow . . . and blow? It gets bigger . . . and bigger . . . and bigger. What happens if you keep blowing, and blowing, and blowing? POP! When it gets too big it bursts with a loud bang!

When we don't fight against pride, the same thing happens. Pride grows bigger and bigger and bigger in our hearts. If it keeps growing and growing, there is a big problem.

> Pride goes before destruction,
>   and a haughty spirit before a fall. (Proverbs 16:18)

We all have pride in our hearts. It is part of our sin nature. Either we can battle against pride, or we can be destroyed by it. Let's see what choice King Uzziah made.

[Uzziah] did what was right in the eyes of the LORD. . . . He set himself to seek God in the days of Zechariah, who instructed him in the fear of God, and as long as he sought the LORD, God made him prosper. (2 Chronicles 26:4–5)

Uzziah "sought the Lord," or depended on God, and God helped him. He won battles against the Philistines and other enemies. He built cities and became very powerful and famous. So Uzziah started to feel a little proud of himself.

He built towers in Jerusalem for defending the city and dug many wells for water. He had many animals, fields, and grape vineyards. Uzziah was an important and rich man. But he did not fight pride. Instead, he let it grow.

His army was large and well trained. They had shields, spears, helmets, coats of armor, bows, and stones for throwing. He was very proud of his army! His pride grew bigger and bigger.

He built machines for the towers that could throw large stones and shoot arrows.

And his fame spread far, for he was marvelously helped, till he was strong. (2 Chronicles 26:15)

Who do you think helped King Uzziah to become famous and strong? It was God. But Uzziah did not praise or thank God. As he became more and more famous, his pride grew and grew and grew.

But when he was strong, he grew proud, to his destruction. For he was unfaithful to the LORD his God. (2 Chronicles 26:16)

Uzziah did not fight pride in his heart, so his pride grew bigger and bigger. He thought he was so important that he went into the temple to burn sweet-smelling incense. Only the priests were supposed to do this, but Uzziah just got angry when the priests reminded him of God's law. King Uzziah's pride puffed him up more and more . . . and then . . . POP! Out came sores on his skin! It was leprosy, which is a very bad disease. Uzziah's pride ended in disaster.

Pride is very dangerous. But if you are a child of God, He can help you to fight this sin in your heart. Only God can give you a truly humble heart. Are you His child? Ask God to help you to fight pride before it grows bigger . . . and bigger . . . and bigger . . . POP!

God opposes the proud but gives grace to the humble. (1 Peter 5:5)

LEARNING TO TRUST GOD

✦ Read about another proud king in the Bible in Daniel 4:28–37. How did Nebuchadnezzar show the pride in his heart? What was the consequence of his pride? What did he learn?

✦ Read 1 Peter 5:5 again. Explain to your mom or dad the difference between being proud and being humble. What does the word *opposes* mean? Think of some responses that will give the glory to God when someone compliments you.

✦ *Activity:* Just for fun, fill some water balloons, making a knot at the mouth. Then have a water balloon fight! Share with each other some ideas for fighting pride in your hearts. Pray and ask God to help you to fight pride.

The Battleground of Rebellion

Have you ever tried to fold a sponge in half? What happens when you let go? It pops back flat. If the sponge could talk, what would it say? Maybe it would say, "I'm *not* going to stay folded up! I want to stretch out, and I *will* get my way!"

When people talk this way, this attitude is called *rebellion*. Rebellion is an attitude of disobedience. It is when our hearts don't want to follow the rules or do what parents, teachers, or someone else in charge asks us to do. Instead, we want to get our own way. Rebellion in the heart is fighting against God and what is right. It is when our hearts say, "No!" to what is right.

Can you think of a rebellious response to these situations?

- Mom says, "You need to change your shirt." A rebellious response might be, "I don't want to," or, "This shirt is fine."

- Dad says, "It is time for bed," but you keep doing whatever you are doing.

- Grandma says, "Would you take out the garbage?" but you ignore her or tell her to ask your brother.

- Your teacher asks you to sit quietly and do your work while she steps out of the room, but you talk to your neighbor or play tic-tac-toe instead.

Rebellion is what Jonah did when God asked him to preach in Nineveh. Do you remember what Jonah did? He got on a boat going *away* from Nineveh! In his heart he wanted to do what he wanted, and so he disobeyed God. He did not want to preach in Nineveh. He wanted his own way instead of God's way.

When you light a match, is it easy to blow the flame out? What if you let the match catch some paper on fire, and then the curtains, and then the kitchen table, and it keeps spreading? Would the fire be easy to blow out then? A very small fire is easy to put out, but a big raging fire is out of control and cannot be easily stopped. Before long, the fire burns up everything around it.

Rebellion works the same way. Small rebellions in the heart are easier to put out than a habit of rebellion that grows and grows and gets out of control. As soon as we feel rebellion in our hearts, we must squash it immediately. We cannot "enjoy" it for a little while, because it quickly gets out of control.

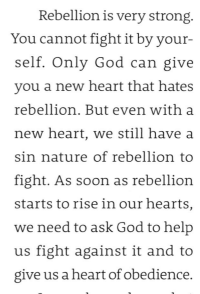

Rebellion is very strong. You cannot fight it by yourself. Only God can give you a new heart that hates rebellion. But even with a new heart, we still have a sin nature of rebellion to fight. As soon as rebellion starts to rise in our hearts, we need to ask God to help us fight against it and to give us a heart of obedience.

Jesus showed us what a heart of obedience looks like. Jesus loved to do what God, His Father, asked Him to do. But God asked Jesus to do something very, very hard. He asked Jesus to go to the cross to pay for sin. Jesus knew he would suffer much pain, loneliness, and sadness on the cross.

Jesus asked His Father if it might be possible to change the plan—to take away the need for Jesus to suffer on the cross.

> He fell on his face and prayed, saying, "My Father, if it be possible, let this cup pass from me; nevertheless, not as I will, but as you will." (Matthew 26:39)

Jesus would not rebel against His Father. He chose to do things His Father's way—He "submitted" to God the Father. He chose His Father's will—what His Father wanted.

Jesus perfectly obeyed His Father and went to the cross. Why do you think He did that? Jesus loves to please His Father. He trusts His Father's wisdom and plan. And He perfectly obeys His Father.

Rebellion is very dangerous. We cannot let it grow in our hearts. Only God can give us a new heart, and only God can help us to fight against rebellion in our hearts. Are you a child of God? Do you love to please your heavenly Father?

> I delight to do your will, O my God;
>   your law is within my heart. (Psalm 40:8)

LEARNING TO TRUST GOD

✣ Read about Jesus' submission to His Father in Matthew 26:36–56. Where do you see Jesus' obedient heart?

✣ Read Proverbs 29:1. What does "stiffens his neck" mean? What is the result of stubborn rebellion?

✣ *Activity:* Examine your heart this week. Were you rebellious or submissive? Confess your rebellion and ask for forgiveness. Thank God for the times that your heart was submissive. Ask Him to give you a submissive heart. Then, as a family, make a special treat. Follow Mom's instructions perfectly. Then eat the treat together![1]

1. Alternate suggestion: Build something with Dad.

The Battleground of Fear

Is fear ever good? Yes, it is good to fear some things. Can you think of some things that are good to fear? A fear of sinning is good. So is a fear of hell, a fear of turning away from God, and a fear of disobedience. These fears are for our protection—just like the fear of running in front of a car. Good fear is fearing the right things. God gives us this fear.

But there is a bad fear called a "spirit of fear" that does not come from God, but from Satan. The spirit of fear is when we see something as greater and more to be feared than the fear of turning from God. It is when our fear of something is bigger than our trust in God.

When a friend suggests doing something wrong and we are afraid to say, "No," that is a spirit of fear. We are more afraid of what our friend will think than what God will think. When something is hard for us to do, and we are afraid to try to do it, that is also a spirit of fear. Our fear of failing is greater than our trust that God will help us. A spirit of fear holds us back from learning new things or having the courage to follow God. A spirit of fear never comes from God.

> For God gave us a spirit not of fear but of power and love and self-control.
> (2 Timothy 1:7)

God does not want us to fear the wrong things. He wants us to have the courage to obey Him.

Do you remember the story of the twelve spies? Joshua and Caleb trusted God. They knew He could give them the land of Canaan. But the other ten spies were controlled by a spirit of fear. They said the people of the land were big—like giants—and they felt like tiny grasshoppers. They looked at the people of

Canaan and were afraid of their size. Their fear was stronger than their trust in God. They were more afraid of what the giant men might do than they were of disobeying God.

But Joshua and Caleb trusted God. They were not afraid of the Canaanites. Instead, they had a good fear of rebelling against God. Fear of rebellion is a good fear. It is given by God to keep us from disobeying Him. It is for our protection.

Satan tempts us to give in to a spirit of fear. But we do not have to give in to temptation. We can fight against it. We fight against it by remembering that God is bigger and stronger than anything else—by trusting in God.

To face a roaring lion would be scary, especially if the lion were hungry! But if that lion were in the zoo and there were a heavy glass window between you and the lion, then you would not be afraid. You would trust that the window would protect you. It would keep the lion away from you.

That is what it means to trust God. Trusting God means truly knowing that He stands between His children and anything that wants to hurt us. It means looking at our strong God instead of at the "lions" we fear.

Do you remember the story of Peter walking on the water? Peter and the disciples were on the lake in a boat. Peter saw Jesus walking on the water toward the boat and wanted to go to Jesus. While looking at Jesus, he stepped out of the boat and started walking. Peter wasn't afraid. He was trusting Jesus.

But then Peter took his eyes off Jesus. He looked at the wind and water around him—it was deep, very deep . . . and Peter gave in to a spirit of fear. He could drown! Peter did not remember Jesus' love and protection over him. Slowly . . . Peter . . . began . . . to . . . sink. His spirit of fear was greater than his trust in Jesus. He was losing the fight of faith in that moment.

He cried out, "Lord, save me." (Matthew 14:30)

And Jesus, who loves to teach His children to trust Him, reached out His hand to Peter. He would not let Peter sink in the water or sink in his faith. He brought Peter safely into the boat.

And those in the boat worshiped him, saying, "Truly you are the Son of God." (Matthew 14:33)

Jesus is the Son of God. He can save you, give you a new heart, and help you to fight against the spirit of fear. Trust in Jesus. He is greater than any fear you have. He is the strong, thick glass between you and all the "roaring lions" in life. Is He your Savior?

When I am afraid,
    I put my trust in you.

In God, whose word I praise,

    in God I trust; I shall not be afraid.

    What can flesh do to me? (Psalm 56:3–4)

LEARNING TO TRUST GOD

✤ Read the story of Jesus saving Peter in Matthew 14:22–33. What does it mean to trust in Jesus? What does it mean to look at the fearful things around us instead of trusting in the greatness and goodness of Jesus?

✤ Read Acts 5:17–42. What was the greater fear of the apostles? What is the fear of man? Why is it important to fear turning away from God?

✤ *Activity:* Do you know someone who needs to know about Jesus, the Son of God and the one who can be trusted in all situations? With your family, think of a way that you can tell this person about the good news of Jesus. Then ask God for the courage to talk to this person. Pray that God will help you to fight a spirit of fear.

The Battleground of Self

If someone is hurt in an accident and a crowd gathers around him, which person would it be most important to let through the crowd—a child with a play doctor kit, or a real doctor? Of course, the most important person in this situation is the real doctor, who might be able to help the hurt man. Wouldn't it be silly for a child to say, "Let me through. I have a play doctor kit"?

But this is something we often do. We think we are the most important. We fail to understand and show that God is most important. We care more about ourselves and what we want than we care about others and what they need.

The battles of unbelief, pride, rebellion, and fear are all fought in the heart. So is the battle of self. The battle against self is one of our biggest battles. This is the battle to make ME smaller or less important. Self says,

What makes ME happy is most important.

The best should be given to ME.

Others should care about ME and my feelings.

What about ME?

The most important person is ME.

Everyone struggles with self. The battle in the heart against self is to stop thinking about ME. When dessert is served, our hearts say, "The big piece should be given to ME." When choosing a game, our hearts scream, "This is the game that is fun for ME. We should play the game I want to play." We do not naturally say, "Whatever my friend wants to play is most important." Each time this battle comes up in the heart, we must fight it. This is not easy to do, and we cannot fight the battle without God's help. Fighting self means that when dessert is passed and our hearts scream, "ME, ME, ME" for the big piece, we must ask God to help us pass the big piece to someone else.

The story of Job will help us understand how to fight the sin of self. Job was a follower of God who suffered much. His enemies stole or killed his animals, his children died when a house fell on them, and then he got sores all over his body. What question do you think Job asked God? He asked, "Why? Why ME?"

Job had a very important lesson to learn. He did not have the right to question what God was doing. He did not understand how small and unimportant he was and how BIG and important God is. He did not understand that he was like the little boy with the doctor kit, and that God is like the real doctor who knows what to do. Job needed to see how great God is.

This is how God answered Job:

Where were you when I laid the foundation of the earth?
Tell me, if you have understanding.
Who determined its measurements— surely you know!
 Or who stretched the line upon it?
. . . .

Have you commanded the morning since your days began, and caused the dawn to know its place,

. . . .

Where is the way to the dwelling of light,
   and where is the place of darkness,

. . . .

Can you send forth lightnings,

. . . .

Do you give the horse his might?

. . . .

Is it by your understanding that the hawk soars
   and spreads his wings toward the south?
Is it at your command that the eagle mounts up
   and makes his nest on high?

. . . .

Shall a faultfinder contend with the Almighty?
   He who argues with God, let him answer it.
     (Job 38:4–5, 12, 19, 35; 39:19, 26–27; 40:2)

What was God telling Job? God was showing Job that He is so much greater than people. He is the great Ruler of the whole world. He made all things and understands all things. He is most important. We do not understand God's wisdom or have the right to complain to God.

Then Job answered the Lord and said:

"Behold, I am of small account; what shall I answer you?
I lay my hand on my mouth." (Job 40:3–4)

What does this verse show about what Job learned? He saw that he was small—so much less important than God, who is greater than all. We fight the sin of self by seeing that God is most important and that we were created to show God's greatness and worth. Our hearts should be screaming not "ME, ME, ME," but *"GOD, GOD, GOD!"* We were created to think not about ourselves, but about God.

In everything we do—whether choosing a game or a piece of dessert—we should ask ourselves, "What brings glory to God? What shows His greatness and worth?" Thinking about self does not bring happiness. If you are a child of God, you will be most happy when you rejoice in God and in what brings Him glory. Are you fighting for ME, ME, ME, or are you living for God's glory?

So, whether you eat or drink, or whatever you do, do all to the glory of God. (1 Corinthians 10:31)

LEARNING TO TRUST GOD

✤ Read 1 Corinthians 10:31 again. Explain to your mom or dad what it means. How can you eat to the glory of God? Do your homework to the glory of God? Treat others to the glory of God?

✤ Read Job 42:1–6. What did Job come to understand? Pray that you too will see the greatness of God and fight the sin of self.

✤ *Activity:* What can your family do to bring glory to God? Think of a project, pray that God's glory will be shown, and then act on your idea.

Never Give Up!

Do you know how many tries it took for Thomas Edison to invent his lightbulb? It was more than 20 . . . more than 100 . . . even more than 1,000! It took more than 10,000 tries! But Thomas Edison never gave up!

Lightbulbs are important—but fighting the fight of faith is so much more important! Are you willing to fight sin 100 times . . . 1,000 times . . . and even more than 10,000 times? Are you willing to believe in God's promises and who He says He is even when things are hard? Will you trust God and stand on His truth even when others do not understand, or when they make fun of you? This is fighting the fight of faith. And we should never give up!

We can learn a lot about not giving up from Thomas Edison. But we can learn even more from Nehemiah about not giving up in the fight of faith.

Do you remember who Nehemiah was? The Jews in Judah were taken captive and sent away to Babylon for seventy years. This happened because they disobeyed God and worshipped idols. Nehemiah was a Jew who served the king in this new land. But Nehemiah was very troubled that the city of Jerusalem was broken down—so troubled that he wept. What should we do when our hearts are so troubled? Nehemiah prayed to God, just as we should do.

Do you know how God answered Nehemiah's prayer? Nehemiah says in the Bible, "The good hand of my God was upon me" (Nehemiah 2:8). God moved the heart of the king to give Nehemiah permission to go back to Jerusalem and rebuild its walls. The king even gave Nehemiah materials for the wall, gates, and a house!

So Nehemiah and the Jews started to build the wall around Jerusalem. Their enemies made fun of them. But Nehemiah prayed to God and did not give up. Then their enemies plotted to fight against the Jews and to make trouble for them. Once again Nehemiah prayed, put some men on guard, and did not give up. They kept building the wall.

But their enemies didn't give up either. They said they would kill the Jews and stop the work. Some of the people of Judah started to complain. But Nehemiah said to them,

> Do not be afraid of them. Remember the Lord, who is great and awesome. (Nehemiah 4:14)

Nehemiah put more men on guard. Half the men carried weapons and half worked on building the wall. Nehemiah did not give up but reminded the people, "Our God will fight for us" (Nehemiah 4:20). The enemies tried to get Nehemiah to leave the work, but he continued to work.

Then his enemies sent a letter saying that they were going to tell the king that the Jews were planning to make Nehemiah the king instead of him. But Nehemiah prayed to God for strength and DID NOT GIVE UP. He and the Jews kept building the wall.

Finally Nehemiah was warned to hide in the temple because his enemies were coming to kill him. But Nehemiah stood firm. He *DID NOT GIVE UP*. He continued building . . . and the Jews finished the wall!

The wall was finished because God helped Nehemiah and the Jews not to give up! Not only were they fighting to finish the wall, but they were also fighting to keep believing that God would help them. They fought the fight of faith and won! The wall was built, and the Jews could live in safety in Jerusalem.

What did the enemies of Judah and God think then?

And when all our enemies heard of it, all the nations around us were afraid and fell greatly in their own esteem, for they perceived that this work had been accomplished with the help of our God. (Nehemiah 6:16)

If you are a Christian, you are also fighting to trust God. Christians fight to believe that God's promises are true and to have the faith that He will always help them. We must fight the fight of faith and *NEVER GIVE UP!*

I have fought the good fight, I have finished the race, I have kept the faith. Henceforth there is laid up for me the crown of righteousness, which the Lord, the righteous judge, will award to me on that Day, and not only to me but also to all who have loved his appearing. (2 Timothy 4:7–8)

LEARNING TO TRUST GOD

✦ Think about the story of Nehemiah. (You may want to read it in Nehemiah 4–6.) What helped Nehemiah to fight the fight of faith?

✦ Read 2 Timothy 4:7–8 again. Then explain the verses in your own words. What is the reward for persevering in faith—for not giving up?

✦ *Activity:* Do an Internet search to learn about Marie Durand, a French Huguenot of the 1700s. What can you learn about persevering in faith from her? Tell someone else her story or put together a book about her life.

The Enemy's Attacks and Spiritual Weapons

Have you ever tried to catch a grasshopper? It's hard, isn't it? Just when you are about to grab it, it jumps away. Sometimes it jumps to the side. Sometimes it jumps to the back. But usually just as you are about to grab it, the grasshopper jumps out of your reach. Do you know why? Because grasshoppers are always watchful and ready.

We need to be watchful and ready too. Satan, our enemy, is always eager to attack us. But if you are a Christian, if you are watchful and ready, you can fight his attacks with God's help. Knowing how the enemy attacks helps us to fight well.

Nehemiah, who never gave up, was watchful and ready. His enemies attacked him in many ways, but he was ready for them. Nehemiah had people as enemies, but Satan was his enemy too. They both attacked Nehemiah and the Jews in many ways.

> Now when Sanballat heard that we were building the wall, he was angry and greatly enraged, and he jeered at the Jews. And he said in the presence of his brothers and of the army of Samaria, "What are these feeble Jews doing? Will they restore it for themselves? Will they sacrifice? Will they finish up in a day? Will they revive the stones out of the heaps of rubbish, and burned ones at that?" Tobiah the Ammonite was beside him, and he said, "Yes, what they are building—if a fox goes up on it he will break down their stone wall!" (Nehemiah 4:1–3)

How did the enemies of the Jews attack them? They made fun of the Jews and insulted them. They said that the Jews were weak or feeble. They tried to discourage the Jews by pointing out how hard the job was—"Will they revive the stones out of the heaps of rubbish . . . ?" But there was more to the attack than this.

For we do not wrestle against flesh and blood, but against the rulers, against the authorities, against the cosmic powers over this present darkness, against the spiritual forces of evil in the heavenly places. (Ephesians 6:12)

The attacks on Nehemiah and the Jews were also spiritual attacks—attacks on their faith. They were attacks by Satan and the spiritual forces of evil. What spiritual battles were Nehemiah and the Jews fighting?

The really important battle was whether Nehemiah and the Jews would believe that God would help them. Would they get discouraged and give up, or would they trust that God was working for them and keep building the wall? The real battle for Nehemiah and the Jews was to fight discouragement, unbelief, and doubt that God was at work, and to fight the temptation to fight back with worldly weapons. Spiritual battles are fought in the heart.

Sometimes we forget that the real battle in any

hard situation is the spiritual battle. The "flesh and blood" battles like the unkind words of Sanballat and Tobiah sometimes make us forget the real battle. So we fight the flesh and blood battle instead. It is very easy to fight the flesh and blood battle with flesh and blood worldly weapons—yelling back insults like,

"Oh yeah! Look who's feeble—you're feeble. In fact, you're wimps!"
"Feeble? I'll show you who's feeble!"
"A fox! Are you kidding? Nothing can break this wall down!"

But Nehemiah was a godly man who fought the spiritual battle with spiritual weapons. Nehemiah fought with prayer.

Hear, O our God, for we are despised. Turn back their taunt on their own heads and give them up to be plundered in a land where they are captives. Do not cover their guilt, and let not their sin be blotted out from your sight, for they have provoked you to anger in the presence of the builders. (Nehemiah 4:4–5)

Nehemiah and the Jews ignored the foolish talk of Sanballat and Tobiah. Instead they prayed and kept working.

So we built the wall. And all the wall was joined together to half its height, for the people had a mind to work. (Nehemiah 4:6)

They did not turn from the job that God gave them. They would not give in to discouragement and unbelief in their hearts. They fought the fight of faith and did not give up!

Everything in life has a spiritual part to it. So all battles are spiritual battles. Spiritual battles can be won only with spiritual weapons. If you are a child of

God, He will help you to fight your spiritual battles with spiritual weapons. Were you watchful and ready for spiritual battles today?

> For though we walk in the flesh, we are not waging war according to the flesh. For the weapons of our warfare are not of the flesh but have divine power to destroy strongholds. (2 Corinthians 10:3–4)

LEARNING TO TRUST GOD

✦ Look at Nehemiah's prayer in Nehemiah 4:4–5. Why did Nehemiah say "they have provoked *you* to anger"? (How were their insults an attack on God?) How is every hard situation or battle we face a spiritual battle?

✦ Read 2 Corinthians 10:3–4 again. Then explain the verses in your own words. Talk as a family about the spiritual battles you faced today. How did you fight them? What worldly weapons could you have used? What spiritual weapons could you have used? Ask God to give you eyes to see the spiritual battles in your life and the faith to fight with spiritual weapons.

✦ *Activity:* In medieval times, coats of arms were used to identify warriors. Each warrior had his own unique coat of arms. Design your own coat of arms that will remind you that your battles are spiritual battles.[1] (A coat of arms usually includes a shield and a banner. You may want to include a verse or verse phrase on your banner.)

---

1. A good resource is *Design Your Own Coat of Arms: An Introduction to Heraldry* by Rosemary A. Chorzempa (Mineola, New York: Dover Publications, 1987).

More of the Enemy's Attacks

Have you ever done a maze puzzle? There are many different paths you can take, but most lead to dead ends. Usually there is only one way that leads to the end of the maze. What do you do when you reach a dead end and there is nowhere else to go? Do you give up? No, you start over and find a different path.

Satan does the same thing in attacking our faith. When one thing doesn't work, he doesn't say, "Oh well, I tried but I couldn't do it. I give up." He is not a quitter, and he does not give up easily. He tries a different way. That's just what he did to Nehemiah and the Jews.

> But when Sanballat and Tobiah and the Arabs and the Ammonites and the Ashdodites heard that the repairing of the walls of Jerusalem was going forward and that the breaches were beginning to be closed, they were very angry. And they all plotted together to come and fight against Jerusalem and to cause confusion in it. (Nehemiah 4:7–8)

Sanballat and Tobiah were being used by Satan to try to stop the building of the wall. They even said that they would kill the Jews. But these were just empty words. They were just trying to scare them. They didn't even attack the Jews. They wanted the Jews to think they had more strength than they really had. They were just bluffing.

Do you know what "bluffing" is? Bluffing is when you trick someone or pretend that something is true when it isn't—like when a basketball player makes another player think he is going one way when he is really going the other way.

Satan does the same thing to us. He tricks us. He wants us to think we should be afraid of him, but that isn't true. He wants us to think he has more power than he really does. Christians have the power of God working for them.

Satan wanted the Jews to be afraid of their enemies. But Nehemiah knew that God is stronger than any enemy. He ignored the enemy's pretend threats, empty words, and bluffing, and he prayed to God. Nehemiah put guards on the lowest part of the wall. Why do you think he put guards there? The easiest place for the enemy to attack is at the weakest spot. So those were the spots that Nehemiah had to protect.

Satan does the same thing. He attacks us where we are weakest. For example, if selfishness is a weakness, you need to protect yourself against it. One way you could do this would be to set aside money to give to the church as soon as you get your allowance. That way you wouldn't be tempted to selfishly spend it on yourself. If fear is your weakness, you might pray every day that God would give you courage. That is protecting your weak spot.

Do you know how Nehemiah fought the attacks of the enemy? He said to the people,

> Do not be afraid of them. Remember the Lord, who is great and awesome. (Nehemiah 4:14)

Nehemiah encouraged the people to "remember the Lord." Instead of thinking of the enemy's strength, Nehemiah told them to remember how great and awesome God is!

Satan looks big and powerful when we are looking at him, but we must look to God who is great and awesome. When we look to God, we realize how small Satan really is. We remember that Satan is just bluffing. Satan does not want us to remember how great God is. He doesn't want us to praise God. In fact, he hates it when we praise God.

If you are a Christian, the greatest way to fight the battle of faith and to defeat the enemy is to remember that God Himself will fight for you. Instead of trying to fight on your own against the wrong things your heart wants to do, ask God to help you.

How do you do this? If someone says something mean to you, and Satan tempts you to say something mean back, you can fight on your own by trying to do what is right. But we are weak and can easily lose the battle. If Jesus is your Savior, you have another choice. You can ask Jesus for help: "Jesus, help me to be forgiving and kind. I am weak. I need your strength. Fight this battle for me."

Then you will have Jesus' strength to fight the battle. When we let God fight our battles, we will have victory because God is strong.

Sometimes we are defeated when we fight the battle alone. When we ask others to join us in the battle, we are stronger. They can join us by praying for us and encouraging us with verses from the Bible and truths about God.

Never give up in the fight of faith. Satan is not a quitter, and we should not be quitters either. God gives His children spiritual weapons to fight sin and Satan. He gives us prayer and verses from the Bible. So don't give up. Don't let Satan bluff you.

Remember the Lord, who is great and awesome. (Nehemiah 4:14)

LEARNING TO TRUST GOD

✤ Read about how Jesus fought Satan in Matthew 4:1–11. How do these verses show you that Satan is persistent—that he doesn't give up? Where did he try to bluff Jesus? How did Jesus fight Satan?

✤ What is an area of weakness for you? Ask Mom or Dad to help you think of a verse to help you fight where you are weak. Memorize the verse. Tell Mom or Dad how you fought the enemy this week.

✤ *Activity:* Watch the part of the 1939 movie *The Wizard of Oz* where the "wizard" attempts to intimidate Dorothy and her friends until he is exposed as a fake. How is Satan like the wizard? How does he try to intimidate Christians? How can we fight him?

Even More of the Enemy's Attacks

Do you like picnics? What is your favorite picnic food? Your favorite might be a favorite for the flies too! They hover around the food, and you shoo them away with your hand. What happens then? The flies come back! You shoo them away again . . . but they come back again. They just won't leave you and your food alone.

Satan does the same thing. He attacks, and you "shoo him away" with Scripture, with prayer, by ignoring him . . . but he keeps coming back.

Remember how Satan attacked Nehemiah and the Jews through Sanballat and Tobiah with their insults, plots, and threats to fight and kill the Jews? Well, after all that, Satan continued to attack Nehemiah. Sanballat and Tobiah sent a message to Nehemiah four times to stop working and meet with them. But each time they asked, Nehemiah refused. He had important work to do, and he would not let them keep him from it. Again, he "shooed Satan away" . . . and again Satan came back, this time with a different plan.

Sanballat sent a messenger to Nehemiah with a letter.

In it was written, "It is reported among the nations . . . that you and the Jews intend to rebel; that is why you are building the wall. And according to these reports you wish to become their king. And you have also set up prophets to proclaim concerning you in Jerusalem, 'There is a king in Judah.' And now the king will hear of these reports. So now come and let us take counsel together." (Nehemiah 6:6–7)

This report was a lie. Nehemiah was not plotting against the king and planning to become king of the Jews. What would Nehemiah do? Would he worry that a message would be sent and that the king would become angry? Would he be afraid of what might happen? Would he stop building the wall? Or would he fight the fight of faith and trust God?

> Then I sent to him, saying, "No such things as you say have been done, for you are inventing them out of your own mind." For they all wanted to frighten us, thinking, "Their hands will drop from the work, and it will not be done." But now, O God, strengthen my hands. (Nehemiah 6:8–9)

Nehemiah recognized the lies and ignored them. He fought the lies with the truth—"No such things as you say have been done, for you are inventing them

out of your own mind." How could Nehemiah be strong enough to speak the truth and fight Satan's attacks of worry and fear? He wasn't. But he knew that his God is a great God. He knew that God is strong and willing to help His people. So Nehemiah asked God to give him His strength. And God did.

It took 52 days for Nehemiah and the Jews to finish the wall, but they finished it! They were attacked many times in different ways, but God gave them the spiritual weapons of prayer, truth, and faith to fight the attacks of Satan. God was faithful to His people. He helped them to build the wall, but even more importantly, He helped them to fight the fight of faith.

God is still faithful to His people today. Satan attacks in many ways and doesn't give up easily. He uses the same attacks on us that he used on Nehemiah. He tries to scare us or make us worry. He attacks us through other people. He tries to make us think he is stronger than he really is, and he lies. But here is the truth about Satan:

He was a murderer from the beginning, and has nothing to do with the truth, because there is no truth in him. When he lies, he speaks out of his own character, for he is a liar and the father of lies. (John 8:44)

Satan is a liar. We cannot believe what he says. Often he will trick us with lies like the following:

"God is not real."
"God will not forgive you."
"It is okay to disobey your mom. She will never find out."
"There is something wrong with you. No one loves you."
"God will not punish us for sin."
"Cheating is all right because this test is dumb."
"You don't have to confess that sin. It is such a small sin."
"Don't ask your brother to forgive you. Make him ask you instead."

If you know the truth from God's Word, you can fight the lies of Satan. Like Nehemiah, you are not strong enough to fight the attacks of Satan on your own. But if you are a child of God, you can ask God to help you and make you strong. Ask Him to help you trust Him and keep you from giving up. When you "shoo" Satan away, just like pesky flies, he will come back . . . again . . . and again. But God will fight for you!

Submit yourselves therefore to God. Resist the devil, and he will flee from you. (James 4:7)

LEARNING TO TRUST GOD

✤ Read Nehemiah 6:15–16. Why were the nations afraid? How did they know that God had helped the Jews? What does seeing the greatness of God show us about ourselves?

✤ Read James 4:6–8. What does being proud look like? Being humble? How do you submit to God? How do you resist the Devil? How do you draw near to God?

✤ *Activity:* Cut stones or bricks from paper. This week as you and your family read the Bible, write verses on the stones/bricks that will help you to fight the fight of faith. Then share the verses with each other and build a "wall of truth" with the stones/bricks on a door or wall in your home.

Battle Strategy: Depend on God

Can you think of a bad situation—like being in a desert without any water, or fighting a lion with a flyswatter? Yikes! Those sound bad! Can you think of any others?

Jehoshaphat was a king of Judah who was in a bad situation. He wasn't facing a lion, but he was facing the army of the Moabites . . . and the Ammonites . . . and the Meunites. Three armies! The Bible says it was a "great multitude." That is a lot of soldiers—and a big problem for Jehoshaphat. The army of Judah was not strong enough to win against their enemies. They needed help—strong help!

What would you do if you were facing huge armies of strong enemies? Would you be afraid like Jehoshaphat was?

> Then Jehoshaphat was afraid and set his face to seek the LORD, and proclaimed a fast throughout all Judah. And Judah assembled to seek help from the LORD; from all the cities of Judah they came to seek the LORD. (2 Chronicles 20:3–4)

The armies of the enemies were stronger than the army of Judah. But Jehoshaphat knew that God is stronger than all the armies of the world. He knew he could depend on our God, who helps His people. So he *stopped*—he stopped worrying—and he *prayed*.

> O LORD, God of our fathers, are you not God in heaven? You rule over all the kingdoms of the nations. In your hand are power and might, so that none is able to withstand you. . . . O our God, will you not execute judgment on them? For we are powerless against this great horde that is coming against us. We do not know what to do, but our eyes are on you. (2 Chronicles 20:6, 12)

Jehoshaphat knew that he and his people were weak, but that God is strong. God rules over all the kingdoms of the world and has all power and might. No army can fight against God and win. So Jehoshaphat looked to God for help. But he didn't rush out with his army to fight the enemy. He and his people "stood before the Lord" (2 Chronicles 20:13). They waited for God to show them what to do.

And the Spirit of the Lord came upon Jahaziel. . . . And he said, "Listen, all Judah and inhabitants of Jerusalem and King Jehoshaphat: Thus says the Lord to you, 'Do not be afraid and do not be dismayed at this great horde, for the battle is not yours but God's. Tomorrow go down against them. . . . You will not need to fight in this battle. Stand firm, hold your position, and see the salvation of the Lord on your behalf, O Judah and Jerusalem.'

Do not be afraid and do not be dismayed. Tomorrow go out against them, and the LORD will be with you." (2 Chronicles 20:14–17)

Then Jehoshaphat and the people of Judah fell down and worshipped God. They praised Him for His power and goodness, for fighting for His people, and for being a faithful God. The next morning the army of Jehoshaphat set out to fight their enemies. Who do you think Jehoshaphat put in the front of the army? The biggest and strongest men? The men with shields? The men on horses?

Jehoshaphat put the singers in the front of the army! They sang praises to God as they marched: "Give thanks to the LORD, for his steadfast love endures forever" (2 Chronicles 20:21). And when they began to praise God, God started a surprise attack on the armies of their enemies. The enemy armies began to fight each other! So when the army of Judah got to the place where God told them to meet the enemy armies, all they found were dead men. There was no one left to fight them! They fought the fight of faith to depend on God, and God worked for them.

We can learn a lot from Jehoshaphat about fighting spiritual battles. We can follow Jehoshaphat's example to STOP, PRAY, and LISTEN. When you are in a spiritual battle,

STOP—Don't just act. Don't just do what you naturally feel like doing. Don't just depend on your own strength.

PRAY—Tell God that you are weak and you need His help. He is strong and wise. Ask God to fight the battle with you. "Not by might, nor by power, but by my Spirit, says the LORD of hosts" (Zechariah 4:6).

LISTEN—Depend on God to show you how to fight the battle. Maybe He will help you to remember a verse from the Bible or send a Christian with wise advice for you. Trust God to help you. "From of old no one has heard or perceived by the ear, no eye has seen a God besides you, who acts for those who wait for him" (Isaiah 64:4).

So, the next time someone cuts in front of you in line, STOP. Don't shove him and say, "Hey, this is my place!" PRAY. "God, I cannot fight my anger. I am weak. Help me. My eyes are on you." Then LISTEN. "Do not repay evil for evil or reviling for reviling, but on the contrary, bless, for to this you were called, that you may obtain a blessing" (1 Peter 3:9). "This is my place, but you may step in front of me."

We cannot fight spiritual battles on our own. We must stop, pray, and listen and depend on God—*for the battle is not ours but God's.*

LEARNING TO TRUST GOD

✦ Read the story of God fighting for Judah in 2 Chronicles 20:1–30. What does this story show you about God? About spiritual battles?

✦ What are some of the battles you face? What would stop, pray, and listen look like in these battles? Give some examples.

✦ *Activity:* Practice stop, pray, and listen this week. Share your experiences with your family. Invite another family or two to pray and sing praises to God together with you.

Battle Strategy: Stand Guard

Do you know what *emphatically* means? It means forcefully, with great strength. Peter said something "emphatically." He said that he would not deny Jesus. He would not turn away from Jesus. He said it forcefully, with great strength. He really meant it . . . but he wasn't strong enough to do it.

Do you remember the story? After the Last Supper, Jesus went to the Mount of Olives with His disciples. He told them that they would "all fall away"—they would all turn away from Him. But Peter didn't believe he would turn away.

Peter said to him, "Even though they all fall away, I will not." (Mark 14:29)

But Jesus knew better. He knew Peter's weakness, the natural sinfulness of Peter's heart, and the shakiness of his faith.

And Jesus said to him, "Truly, I tell you, this very night, before the rooster crows twice, you will deny me three times." (Mark 14:30)

Three times! Peter was sure this would not happen. He would never leave Jesus. He would never turn away, no matter what!

He said emphatically, "If I must die with you, I will not deny you." And they all said the same. (Mark 14:31)

Peter was sure he would stand with Jesus, and so were the other disciples. They would never leave Jesus. They would always stick with him. They were very sure of themselves. But Jesus knew they were not as strong as they thought they were.

He took Peter, James, and John to pray with Him in Gethsemane and asked them to keep watch while He went to pray. When Jesus came back an hour later, the disciples were asleep.

And he came and found them sleeping, and he said to Peter, "Simon, are you asleep? Could you not watch one hour? Watch and pray that you may not enter into temptation. The spirit indeed is willing, but the flesh is weak." (Mark 14:37–38)

Jesus knew they would be tempted to turn away from Him. They would be tempted to care more about themselves than about Jesus. So Jesus asked them to watch—be on guard—and pray. But they couldn't do it, not even for an hour. Two more times Jesus went to pray . . . and two more times He came back to find

the disciples asleep. They were not on guard. They were not praying. They were not strong enough to obey Jesus or wise enough to pray for strength.

As Jesus was speaking, a crowd came with swords and clubs, and they grabbed Jesus. What do you think Peter did? Remember that Peter *emphatically* said he would die for Jesus. What did the disciples, who all said they would never deny Jesus, do?

And they all left him and fled. (Mark 14:50)

All of them, every one of them, left Jesus and fled. They ran away. They did not stay with Jesus. They did not stand up for Him. They turned and ran away from Jesus.

How very sad this is. It is sad because the disciples were not strong enough in faith to trust God and stand strong with Jesus. But it is also sad because we would probably do the same thing. When we are tempted to be afraid, think only of ourselves, or be safe instead of being loyal, we too sin. Just like the disciples, we fail to watch and pray for ourselves—to pray that we would be strong in faith, that we would not sin, that we would follow Jesus anywhere. We think we are stronger than we really are.

How foolish it is to think, "I can handle it. I can hang around a bad crowd of kids." Or, "It's okay if I skip having my Bible time. I am strong. I don't need to fight for my faith."

Instead, we should pray every day, "Jesus, I am weak, but you are strong. I need you. Make my faith strong. Keep me from sin. Help me to love you more than I love the world." That is watching over or standing guard over our soul. That is depending on Jesus and not on ourselves. The way to keep believing is to watch and pray—to stand guard.

Do you know that a policeman is always watching, always on guard—even when he is not working? He notices what is going on around him. He might be in a restaurant talking with a friend, but at the same time he is noticing the people around him. He sees who comes in and who leaves. Often he will not sit with his back to the door or to the other tables. He sits where he can see most of the restaurant. He is always on the lookout.

This is the same way we need to be in our spiritual lives. We need to be always on the lookout for things that would hurt our faith, pay attention to how things affect our hearts, and pray that God will give us strength.

Do you know why we need to do this? We need to be on guard because Satan is a strong enemy. He is always on the lookout for a way to get at us. He is always trying to attack our faith. So be on guard. Admit that you need God and ask for His strength.

Be sober-minded; be watchful. Your adversary the devil prowls around like a roaring lion, seeking someone to devour. (1 Peter 5:8)

LEARNING TO TRUST GOD

✢ Read about Jesus and the disciples in Mark 14:26–50. Explain verse 38. How are you weak? Pray that God will make your faith strong.

✢ Read 1 Peter 5:8. How is Satan like a lion? Why does Satan want to devour us? How does he devour us? What does being "sober-minded" and "watchful" look like in our spiritual lives?

✢ *Activity:* Go on a short drive. Notice what is around you. What do you see that is helpful to your faith? Why is it helpful? What things are not helpful to your faith? Why are they not helpful? What can you do to be more watchful over your soul?

Battle Strategy: Be Prepared

Can someone just decide to become a pilot, get in a plane, and fly away? What does he have to do first? He needs special training and many hours of practice. A soldier needs special training too. He has to march for miles to build up his physical strength. He has to practice shooting at targets and learn how to use special equipment. It takes hard work for pilots and soldiers to be prepared to do their jobs.

We have to work hard to be prepared to fight the fight of faith too. We never know when an attack will come, but when the attack does come, we must be ready. At that point, it is too late to prepare.

Jesus showed us how to be prepared and ready to fight spiritual battles. Jesus is God, and when Jesus came to earth He also became a man. That means He got hungry and tired just like us.

Before Jesus started his work of teaching and healing, He faced a fierce spiritual battle. He did not eat for forty days, and He was very hungry. How hungry do you think Jesus was?

Satan always looks for our weak spots, and he knew that Jesus was hungry. So Satan tempted Jesus to turn the stones into bread to eat. What did Jesus do?

But he answered, "It is written,

'Man shall not live by bread alone,
   but by every word that comes from the mouth of God.'"
      (Matthew 4:4)

Where was this written? In the Bible, in the book of Deuteronomy.[1] How did Jesus fight Satan's suggestion? He fought using the Word of God. He knew exactly what to say. Jesus was prepared by having the verse memorized.

What did Satan do next? He didn't give up. He is like a prowling lion looking for another weak spot and another way to attack. So Satan took Jesus to the highest point of the temple in Jerusalem . . .

1. Deuteronomy 8:3

and said to him, "If you are the Son of God, throw yourself down, for it is written,

> 'He will command his angels concerning you,'

and

> 'On their hands they will bear you up,
> lest you strike your foot against a stone.' " (Matthew 4:6)

Satan used God's Word to attack Jesus. But Satan is a liar and a deceiver. He did not use the Bible rightly. Satan tried to make it say something that was not true. Satan tried to get Jesus to prove that He is the Son of God. But Jesus did not have a heart of pride, and He was ready for Satan's attack.

> Jesus said to him, "Again it is written, 'You shall not put the Lord your God to the test.' " (Matthew 4:7)

How did Jesus fight the fight of faith? Did Jesus say, "I wonder if I should throw myself down? What is the right thing to do? There must be something in the Word of my Father that will help me."? Did Jesus say, "Just a minute, let me go inside the temple and check the scrolls?" No! Jesus knew the Scriptures very well. He knew that Satan was twisting God's Word, and He was ready to fight the battle using the Word of God.

Still Satan did not give up. He took Jesus to a high mountain where Jesus could see all the land around. Satan promised Jesus all the kingdoms of the world if Jesus would bow down and worship him.

> Then Jesus said to him, "Be gone, Satan! For it is written,

'You shall worship the Lord your God
 and him only shall you serve.'" (Matthew 4:10)

Over and over, Jesus fought Satan's attack, using the Word of God. He was ready with His spiritual weapon. He stood firm against Satan, and finally Satan left Him alone . . . for a while.

If you are a child of God, you have the same weapon as Jesus—the powerful Word of God. But you must be prepared. You must work hard to know the Bible and memorize verses. Then God's Word will be with you all the time, and you will be ready to fight the fight of faith.

Are you memorizing Bible verses? Are you prepared for spiritual battles with spiritual weapons?

I have stored up your word in my heart,
 that I might not sin against you. (Psalm 119:11)

LEARNING TO TRUST GOD

✤ Read about Jesus' fight of faith in Matthew 4:1–11. What sins did Satan tempt Jesus to do? What can you learn about fighting temptation and spiritual battles from Jesus?

✤ Read Psalm 119:9–16. How does the writer feel about God's Word? What can you learn about fighting the fight of faith from these verses?

✤ *Activity:* If your family is not memorizing Scripture, make a plan to do so and start memorizing this week.[2] Write a note using Scripture to encourage someone.

---

2. You may want to consider using the Fighter Verse memory program from Children Desiring God, www.children desiringgod.org

Battle Strategy: Resist the Enemy

Have you ever arm wrestled? If not, try it with someone right now. When the other person tries to push your arm in one direction, what do you do? You resist. You refuse to be pushed in that direction. Instead you push the other way.

This is a good reminder of how to fight the fight of faith. Satan tries to push us away from God and toward sin. We can either let him, or we can say, "No!" and refuse to be pushed. We can resist him like Joseph did.

Joseph was a Hebrew slave in the house of an Egyptian named Potiphar. He was a trusted slave and was in charge of Potiphar's whole household. But there was one problem: Joseph was also very handsome, and this caught the interest of Potiphar's wife. She wanted Joseph to treat her like she was his wife. But Joseph refused. It was against God's law, and it would destroy his master's trust in him. He resisted sin and Satan's temptation, and he trusted the commands of God and believed His promises. He was faithful to his master Potiphar and to God, his greater Master.

> He is not greater in this house than I am, nor has he kept back anything from me except yourself, because you are his wife. How then can I do this great wickedness and sin against God? (Genesis 39:9)

But Potiphar's wife kept tempting Joseph "day after day" (Genesis 39:10). She did not give up. Joseph knew that what she asked him to do was wrong. He kept refusing and resisting her invitation to sin. Finally, one day when she was alone in the house with Joseph, Potiphar's wife grabbed Joseph by his cloak. But Joseph was on guard and prepared. He wriggled out of his cloak and ran away from her.

He was determined not to sin against his God. In his heart he wanted to please God and do the right thing.

> Great peace have those who love your law;
>> nothing can make them stumble. (Psalm 119:165)

Joseph did not stumble. Joseph gave us a good example of how to stand firm and resist sin. He resisted sin and Satan because the desires of his heart were godly.

He loved God and wanted to please Him. If you have godly heart desires, you can resist sin and Satan too.

Think about your favorite candy. Suppose it is almost suppertime and your mother says that you cannot have any candy before supper. You walk into the kitchen and see a piece of your favorite candy on the counter. How can you respond to the temptation to eat the candy?

You could immediately walk out of the kitchen or put the candy in a drawer where you wouldn't have to look at it. Or you could smell the candy, unwrap it, smell it again, and then lick it. Do you think it would be hard to resist the candy now?

The best way to resist sin and Satan is to resist immediately—as soon as we are tempted. When we "play" with temptation, it is harder for us to resist. We must resist immediately and flee or run away from sin like Joseph did. What helps us most to do this is having a godly heart desire—to love what is right and pleasing to God.

> Your testimonies are wonderful;
> therefore my soul keeps them. (Psalm 119:129)

Suppose you have a spelling test in school, and one of the words is *requirement*. You don't know how to spell *requirement*, but you remember seeing this word on a poster on your classroom wall. You can either cheat and look at the poster, or try to spell the word on your own. How do you fight the fight of faith in this situation?

It starts with a GODLY HEART DESIRE—the desire to be an honest, trustworthy person who wants to please God. Then you must RESIST IMMEDIATELY. Ask God for help, and in your heart determine, "I'm not going to cheat. It is better to be honest and to please God than to get a good grade." This is believing the truth. It is resisting sin and trusting God.

The next step is to FLEE FROM SIN. Turn away from the poster and write the word *requirement* on your spelling test. You might not spell the word right, but you have won the battle of trusting God. You have fought the fight of faith and have won!

When you have a *godly heart desire*, and you *resist immediately* and *flee from sin*, you are winning the fight of faith. You are trusting in God's ways and in His Word. You are loving God and hating sin. You are pleasing God and watching over your soul. And God's wonderful promise for you follows:

> Submit yourselves therefore to God. Resist the devil, and he will flee from you. (James 4:7)

LEARNING TO TRUST GOD

✦ Read Genesis 39:1–12. What were Joseph's godly heart desires? How did he fight the fight of faith? Ask God to give you godly heart desires and to help you fight the fight of faith.

✦ Read Psalm 119:129–136. What are the heart desires of the writer of this psalm? How is he fighting the fight of faith?

✦ *Activity:* This week ask God to help you to have godly heart desires, resist immediately, and flee from sin. Then share your experiences with your family. What truths helped you? What made fighting the fight of faith hard? How can you support and encourage each other? Do one practical thing to encourage your family in the fight of faith.

Battle Strategy: Renew Your Mind

What happens to your shoes when you walk through a muddy place? Your shoes get muddy, don't they? They are still shoes, but they are shoes with mud on them.

Do you know that Christians are like those muddy shoes? The Bible says,

Now we have received not the spirit of the world, but the Spirit who is from God, that we might understand the things freely given us by God. (1 Corinthians 2:12)

Christians have the Holy Spirit—the Spirit who is from God—in us. So we think differently from people who don't have the Holy Spirit. We also love different things. We love God and the Bible and righteousness. We don't love sin. That makes us different from other people.

But Christians live in this broken, sinful world. And that means that we "get mud" on our souls—the desires and thinking of this world sticks to us sometimes. Sometimes we don't even notice it, but the wrong thinking and the wrong desires of the world affect us. This happened to Peter.

Jesus told the disciples that He would suffer many things and then be killed. After three days He would rise from the dead. But Peter wasn't thinking in god-like ways. He was thinking like the world. He didn't understand that Jesus had to die. He thought that Jesus was wrong.

Could Jesus ever be wrong? No! But Peter didn't realize that the world's "mud" had rubbed off on his thinking. So Peter scolded Jesus. Can you imagine scolding Jesus? Well, that is just what Peter did. He thought Jesus was wrong and should not say such things.

But Jesus understood the plan of God. He thought in godlike ways, and He wanted what God, the Father, wanted; He had a godly heart desire.

But turning and seeing his disciples, he rebuked Peter and said, "Get behind me, Satan! For you are not setting your mind on the things of God, but on the things of man." (Mark 8:33)

Jesus knew that Peter wasn't thinking rightly. Peter wasn't thinking about what was best in God's plan to save sinners; he was thinking about what he wanted. He did not want Jesus to die. He wanted Jesus to be a conquering king.

It is very easy for us to believe Satan's lies and to think in ways that are different from what the Bible teaches. So we must read the Bible often and change our worldly thinking to think God's thoughts. We need to "brush the mud" of the world off our minds and hearts. We must be the people of God, not people who love the world. This is part of the fight of faith.

> Do not be conformed to this world, but be transformed by the renewal of your mind, that by testing you may discern what is the will of God, what is good and acceptable and perfect. (Romans 12:2)

We need to brush off the world's influence. We need to get rid of the ways in which the world's thinking sticks to us. We need to make our minds like new again. If we think rightly—like the Bible teaches—we will spot the lies of Satan more easily.

God's Word, the Bible, shows us the right way of thinking. But if we don't read it often and think about what it says, we won't think like the Bible. We need to ask questions when we read the Bible—questions like, What does this word mean? What does this verse really say? Does the way I understand this verse make sense with the rest of what the Bible teaches? What does this verse teach me about how to live in a way that pleases God?

We need to look at our lives and ask if we are thinking like the Bible teaches. We need to "test" what we are thinking. Is the way we think about right and wrong what the world teaches, or is it what the Bible teaches? The world might say that it is all right to keep too much change when a cashier makes a mistake. But the Bible says that taking something that doesn't belong to us is stealing, and stealing is wrong. What do you think about keeping too much change? Do your actions show that you believe the truth of the Bible?

If you are a Christian, you have received the Holy Spirit, who helps you to understand God's truth. But if you are not a Christian, you do not have any protection against the lies of Satan. You cannot "renew your mind," and you will not be able to judge what is "good and acceptable and perfect" in different situations. You will not be able to do the will of God and walk in God's good ways. How important it is to trust Jesus as your Savior and have the Holy Spirit's protection!

> Do not love the world or the things in the world. If anyone loves the world, the love of the Father is not in him. For all that is in the world—the desires of the flesh and the desires of the eyes and pride in possessions— is not from the Father but is from the world. And the world is passing away along with its desires, but whoever does the will of God abides forever. (1 John 2:15–17)

LEARNING TO TRUST GOD

✤ Read 1 Corinthians 2:12–16. What is the "spirit of the world"? Who is the "natural person"? How can you receive the "Spirit who is from God"?

✤ Read Romans 12:2 again. What does it mean to be "conformed to this world" and to be "transformed by the renewal of your mind"? How can you "test" your thoughts?

✤ *Activity:* As a family, look at some of the messages that you receive (e.g., advertisements, television programs, articles, books) and test them to see how they compare to the teaching of the Bible. Pray that God will give you discernment and a heart to seek and trust the truth.

Battle Strategy: Dwell on the Truth

Do you like guessing games? Guess what animal I am thinking of. It gives us milk. It has four legs and a tail, and it lives on a farm. The letter *o* is in its name. What is it? Can you make its sound?

What helped you to decide what animal it is? It was the clues you read, which were put into your mind. So your thinking influenced your action—determined what sound you made. Did you make a mooing sound? The sound—your action—came from thinking of a cow.

So "*input*," what we "put in" our minds, affects our *thinking*, which affects our *actions*. So if you want to do what is right, you must first think rightly. If you want to think rightly, you must put truth into your mind. That is why the Bible tells us,

> Finally, brothers, whatever is true, whatever is honorable, whatever is just, whatever is pure, whatever is lovely, whatever is commendable, if there is any excellence, if there is anything worthy of praise, think about these things. (Philippians 4:8)

The things we put into our minds are the things that will fill our thoughts. The Bible is telling us to put good things into our minds so our minds will dwell or think on good things. We should be careful not to put in bad things and be sure to put the best things into our minds.

Our minds are like a computer screen. What happens to the screen if you don't use it for a few minutes? Usually a screen saver appears. Whatever you put into your computer as your screen saver is what appears when your computer is idle—when it isn't being used. If we put bubbles on the screen saver, bubbles will come up, not airplanes. If we use a blank screen as the screen saver, no funny shapes will come up at all.

It works the same way with our minds. Whatever we put into our minds is what will come back into them when they are idle—when we aren't consciously using them. If you put in Bible verses, then those verses come into your mind when you are riding in the car, waiting for the bus, or doing your chores and not thinking about anything in particular. If you put junk into your mind, then when you are not actively using your mind you will dwell on junk.

It is dangerous to put junk into our minds because junk in the mind will cause our hearts to desire junk. King Solomon married many foreign women. They did not worship the God of Israel. They worshipped idols, and they put their "junk" ideas about idols into Solomon's mind.

For when Solomon was old his wives turned away his heart after other gods, and his heart was not wholly true to the Lord his God, as was the heart of David his father. (1 Kings 11:4)

Because Solomon was not careful to put true, honorable, just, pure, lovely, commendable, excellent, or praiseworthy things into his mind, he did not dwell on these good things. And this changed his heart and turned it away from God.

When Goliath challenged the army of Israel, the men were scared. They thought about how big and tough Goliath was. Instead of having hearts of bravery, they were filled with fear. Their fearful thinking led to the action of running away from Goliath.[1]

But David's mind was filled with other thoughts.

And David said, "The Lord who delivered me from the paw of the lion and from the paw of the bear will deliver me from the hand of this Philistine." (1 Samuel 17:37)

Then David said to the Philistine, "You come to me with a sword and with a spear and with a javelin, but I come to you in the name of the Lord of hosts, the God of the armies of Israel, whom you have defied. This day the Lord will deliver you into my hand, and I will strike you down and cut off your head. And I will give the dead bodies of the host of the Philistines this day to the birds of the air and to the wild beasts of the earth, that all the earth may know that there is a God in Israel, and that all this assembly may know that the Lord saves not with sword and spear. For the battle is the Lord's, and he will give you into our hand." (1 Samuel 17:45–47)

1. 1 Samuel 17:24

David's thinking led him to trust the Lord and face the giant, Goliath. He was filled with confidence in God, not fear. Where did his thinking come from? It came from filling his mind day after day with the truth about God as he sang while watching his sheep. It came from dwelling on or thinking about the truth. By choosing to dwell on the truth, David was prepared for the spiritual battle against fear. He was prepared to trust God and fight Goliath.

What we put into our minds will affect our thinking and then our actions. So we must be careful to constantly put the truth into our minds and dwell on the truth. We must test everything to make sure it agrees with the Bible, because it is easy to be deceived or fooled.

By the way, the correct sound for our guessing game is "maa maa." The four-legged farm animal with an *o* in its name that gives us milk also has a beard. It is a goat. Our minds are easily led along by what we most think about, aren't they?

If then you have been raised with Christ, seek the things that are above, where Christ is, seated at the right hand of God. Set your minds on things that are above, not on things that are on earth (Colossians 3:1–2)

LEARNING TO TRUST GOD

✦ Read Philippians 4:8 again. Make sure you understand all the words. What would be good to put in your mind? How will you do that?

✦ Read Psalm 29. How would dwelling on this psalm give confidence in God?

✦ *Activity:* David sang his psalms and dwelt on the truth of who God is. Singing is a good way to memorize Scripture. Choose a verse from fighter-verses.com to help you fight the fight of faith. Then learn the song for that verse. If your family is musical, you can also play and sing the song. Dwell on Scripture this week by singing the song.

Battle Strategy: Do Not Compromise

Imagine a beautiful garden. What is in this garden? Does it have flowers, bushes, a big climbing tree, a bench, a fountain, a walkway, birds, or a swing? The Bible talks about a garden too.

> I passed by the field of a sluggard,
>   by the vineyard of a man lacking sense,
> and behold, it was all overgrown with thorns;
>   the ground was covered with nettles,
>   and its stone wall was broken down. (Proverbs 24:30–31)

Does this sound like the garden you imagined? How did this man's garden become such a mess? The man who owned the garden was lazy and foolish, so he did not take care of his garden. Since he didn't pull up the weeds, little weeds grew into big weeds and choked out the pretty flowers or vegetables. The stone wall began to fall apart, and he didn't fix it. This didn't happen in a day or even a week. Little by little, over time, the garden fell into ruin until all its beauty . . . and everything good in it . . . was gone.

Our hearts are like gardens. The beautiful flowers and bushes are like our love for God and the work of His goodness in us. If we want our heart gardens to be beautiful, we must take care of them. We must plant good seeds in our heart gardens—like seeds of renewing our minds and dwelling on the truth.

Our enemy, Satan, blows weed seeds of temptation to sin into our heart gardens. Seeds that begin to grow into weeds need to be pulled immediately. We must stand watch diligently over our hearts and be prepared for sin seeds and weeds. We must resist Satan's seed sowing and the weeds that grow from these seeds.

What happens if we are lazy and foolish like the man in the Bible verse? We do not pull out the sin weeds that grow in our hearts. We let them grow, and little sins will become big sins. Every sin weed crowds out our love for God and the work of His goodness in our hearts. If we continue to let sin grow, the weeds of sin will choke out our love for God, and our hearts will look like the garden in Proverbs—overgrown with thorns, covered with prickly plants, and surrounded by a broken-down wall. Our hearts will not be pretty or good.

What kind of heart do you want? Do you want a pure heart like a beautiful garden, or a sin-filled heart? If you trust in Jesus, He will help you to fight the sin weeds in your heart. Let Him help you to pull them out by turning away from sin. Ask Him to give you a heart that loves God and what is right. Ask Him to help you not to compromise.

Do you know what *compromise* means? Compromising is agreeing to give up the best for something that is not as good. Compromising our love for God in return for sin is very foolish and very dangerous.

When a traffic light turns yellow, it is a warning that the light will soon turn red. There is a signal light for sin compromises too. Whenever you feel that sin isn't so bad, or that small sins are not important, or that you can handle something that could hurt your soul, it is a signal that you are making a bad compromise. Do you ever say words like these?

"It's no big deal."
"I can handle it. This won't affect me."
"It's not that bad" or "There's nothing really wrong with it. Everyone else is doing it."
"I don't have to be perfect. Everyone sins, so I can too."

Saying these words might be a signal that you are compromising. You might be ignoring the sin seeds in the garden of your heart.

Maybe you think that watching one bad movie is "no big deal." But it *is* a big deal. It's serious because the Bible teaches us to be pure. It's a big deal because little things grow into big things. Next time you might watch something worse. Or you might watch the bad part over and over in your mind. Each time that happens, your purity is attacked and sin grows in your heart.

How can you pull up that sin weed? Begin by telling God about your sin, and repent or turn away from that sin. Pray something like this:

"God, I was so foolish. I did not stand guard over my heart. I watched something I shouldn't have watched, and it put bad pictures and awful language into my mind. I am so sorry for offending You in that way. Please forgive me for my sin."

That is a good place to start. Then decide to be more careful and obedient. The next time you have the choice to watch something that could hurt your soul, ask Jesus to help you. Finally, resist the enemy, refuse to compromise, and run from sin.

What kind of garden is growing in your heart? Is it filled with beautiful flowers of love for God and a desire for what is good and right? Or are there weeds growing bigger and bigger? Will you ask Jesus to help you not to compromise and keep you from trading the wonderful love for God in return for the weeds of sin?

> Keep your heart with all vigilance,
>> for from it flow the springs of life.
> Put away from you crooked speech,
>> and put devious talk far from you.
> Let your eyes look directly forward,
>> and your gaze be straight before you.
> Ponder the path of your feet;
>> then all your ways will be sure.
> Do not swerve to the right or to the left;
>> turn your foot away from evil. (Proverbs 4:23–27)

LEARNING TO TRUST GOD

✤ Read Proverbs 4:23–27 again. Explain this verse to Mom or Dad. What does this verse tell you about not compromising?

✤ Is there any way you are compromising your heart? Is there anything you need to confess? How can you turn from sin? Ask Jesus to help you not to compromise your heart.

✤ *Activity:* Plant some seeds (grass in a cup or flowers in a garden)[1]. How will you care for your plants? Or visit a beautiful garden or a neglected garden. Talk about how the garden was cared for and how that relates to caring for our hearts.

---

1. If you plant a garden, you may want to let some weeds grow in a section to see what happens to the plants.

Battle Strategy: Confession

Have you ever tasted sour milk? Yuck! It is bad! The milk can look fine, but when you taste it, you find out that it really isn't fine at all.

Our hearts can be like the sour milk. They seem fine, but there is sin living in our hearts. Until we take a closer look, we might not even realize the sin is there.

For us to keep sin from growing, it is important to check our hearts closely and often. But sometimes, even when we check our hearts, we don't see our own sin. What can we do? The Bible has a good suggestion.

> Search me, O God, and know my heart!
>   Try me and know my thoughts!
> And see if there be any grievous way in me,
>   and lead me in the way everlasting! (Psalm 139:23–24)

Because we can't always see what is in our hearts, we must ASK GOD to show us our hidden sins. How does God show us our sin?

Sometimes He shows us through the Bible. A verse can prick our hearts and show us how we have sinned. Sometimes God shows us our sin through another person—like when He sent Nathan to tell David about his sin. Sometimes He shows us by letting us get caught in our sin—like when a teacher catches someone cheating on a test.

What is the next step in fighting the fight of faith and getting rid of sin in our hearts? Well, if you drank something poisonous would you say, "I have other things to do, so I think I will go to the doctor next Thursday"? Of course not! What would you do? You would rush to the hospital immediately. The poison is dangerous and you must get it out of your body as fast as you can.

Sin is dangerous too—very dangerous. Do you remember about the weeds in the garden of our hearts? If we don't pull them right away, they grow and choke out our love for God and what is right. So when God shows us a sin in our hearts, do you think we should we say, "I can wait and confess this later," or, "There are so many ways that I don't sin, so I don't need to worry about this one"? No! A wise person will CONFESS IMMEDIATELY.

Confessing is not just quickly telling God, "I'm sorry for my sin." Confessing means we have true sorrow over our sin. We know how awful our sin is to our good and holy God. Confessing sin in a way that pleases God means we are truly ashamed and saddened by our sin. In our hearts we want Jesus to forgive us and take away the shame of our sin.

Do you know how to confess your sin? There is no one right way to do it. The most important thing is what is in your heart. Here is one way to confess sin:

First, admit your sin specifically, telling God what you did. For example, "God, I lied when I told my mom that my home-work was done," or, "I was selfish when I wouldn't share my markers with my sister."

Next, ask God to forgive you. King David gave us an example of this in the Bible: "Hide your face from my sins, and blot out all my iniqui-ties" (Psalm 51:9).

Then ask God to help you to turn from your sin. This might mean uncovering your sin, like telling your mom that you lied about your homework. Or it might mean turning away from selfishness and toward generosity by letting your sister use your markers. This is turning from sin and doing what you can to right the wrong you did. Then you could pray with David, "Create in me a clean heart, O God, and renew a right spirit within me" (Psalm 51:10).

It is so wonderful to have a heart that wants to confess immediately. God is pleased by a heart that hates sin and truly wants to get rid of it. You truly repent when your heart hates your sin and when you make the decision to TURN FROM SIN.

How often do you brush your teeth? Two or three times a day? Why? Because tiny living things called bacteria stick to your teeth. They cause staining and cavities. Bacteria is not the only thing that sticks to you. Every day the "mud" of the world sticks to your soul. So how often should you confess sin? Only on Christmas and Easter? Only on communion Sundays? Every Sunday? Or every day? Every day we sin, and every day we need to pull the seeds of sin from our hearts. It feels good to have clean teeth, but it is so much more wonderful to have a clean conscience.

If we confess our sins, he is faithful and just to forgive us our sins and to cleanse us from all unrighteousness. (1 John 1:9)

LEARNING TO TRUST GOD

✛ Read Psalm 51:1–17. What can you learn about confession from this psalm? Is there anything you need to confess?

✛ Read 1 John 1:9 again. Explain what confession is. Why is God "just to forgive us our sins"? What does it mean to "cleanse us from all unrighteousness"?

✛ *Activity:* As a family, get new toothbrushes. Every time you brush your teeth, use it as a reminder to ask God to show you the uncleanness in your heart. You may also want to write your own psalm of confession and repentance like David did in Psalm 51.

Battle Strategy: Demolish Strongholds

Have you ever helped someone pull weeds? Are some weeds harder to pull up than others? Why? Small, new weeds have weak roots, but weeds that have been growing for a while have long, strong roots that go deep into the ground. They have a *strong hold* on the dirt. Sometimes the roots even curl around other plant roots. So it takes a lot of strength and ripping away to pull them up.

The same thing happens when we let a seed of sin grow in our hearts so that it becomes a large weed of sin. Its roots take hold of our hearts and become longer and stronger. As it grows, it curls around other things in our lives until that sin has a very strong hold on our hearts. Sin that we allowed to grow a long time is called a "stronghold." The sin started small, but it grew and grew until it has become very hard to control.

Can you think of a sin that could become a stronghold? How about lying? If you lie and immediately confess your sin and turn away from it, lying does not grow in your heart. But if you lie and ignore the uncomfortable feeling it gives you, and then make excuses for lying instead of confessing your sin, you give lying room to grow in your heart. Then you are tempted to lie again to cover up the first lie. You continue to ignore your conscience. More temptations to lie come, and you do not resist sin and Satan. Soon lying becomes a habit. Lies just pop out of your mouth when you are in a difficult spot. The sin becomes a habit and a stronghold. It has a strong hold on our hearts, and it is difficult to destroy.

But strongholds can be destroyed. God gave us a picture of how to destroy sin strongholds when Israel destroyed Jericho—another kind of stronghold. Jericho was a well-protected city surrounded by a tall, thick, strong wall. Do you remember how Israel destroyed Jericho?

The Israelites marched around Jericho for six days. They showed the people of Jericho that they were serious about taking their city. Do you remember what happened on the seventh day? They marched around the city seven times. The priests blew the trumpets and the people shouted that the Lord had given them the victory! Then the strong, unbreakable walls of Jericho *tumbled down*. The Israelites entered the city and destroyed everything.

This is the way sin strongholds are destroyed. First we must "march" against Satan. We must show that we are serious about destroying the stronghold by uncovering sin and not hiding it anymore. Marching against the stronghold of lying means deciding to destroy it and confessing it to God and to your parents.

Sin's stronghold is destroyed with the power of God just like God destroyed the walls of Jericho. We cannot do it in our own strength. We must "shout" to God for help.

> For the weapons of our warfare are not of the flesh but have divine power to destroy strongholds. (2 Corinthians 10:4)

We have the spiritual weapons of prayer, the Word of God, and the power of God. If we dwell on the truth and depend on Jesus, our sin will be given a powerful blow. A stronghold of lying is destroyed by asking Jesus every day to help you tell the truth, calling on Him when you are tempted to lie, and depending on Him to help you.

We must completely "destroy" sin, just like Israel completely destroyed Jericho. We cannot leave any little part of the sin stronghold in our lives. Sin is so dangerous that we should do anything to destroy it.

> If your right eye causes you to sin, tear it out and throw it away. For it is better that you lose one of your members than that your whole body be thrown into hell. And if your right hand causes you to sin, cut it off and throw it away. For it is better that you lose one of your members than that your whole body go into hell. (Matthew 5:29–30)

We must MARCH against the strongholds in our lives, SHOUT to God for His strength and help, and DESTROY the sin completely.

Living with a stronghold of sin is like being tied with a rope. When you are tied up, you can't raise your arms, or scratch an itch. You can't put on a jacket when you are cold or get a cool drink when you are hot.

Strongholds tie us up too. They keep us from growing in faith. They keep us from doing good things. And they steal our joy and peace. They are like ropes that tie us up. But Jesus wants to give us something better. He came to rip out all the strongholds of sin! He came to set our hearts free from the power of sin. Do you want this freedom?

For freedom Christ has set us free; stand firm therefore, and do not submit again to a yoke of slavery. (Galatians 5:1)

LEARNING TO TRUST GOD

✤ Read Proverbs 6:27–28. What does this tell you about the danger of sin? Are there any strongholds in your life?

✤ Explain Matthew 5:29–30 to your mom or dad.

✤ *Activity:* Have a snowball, water balloon, or rolled-up socks fight. Fight with vigor! Then talk about how aggressively we must fight against sin. What things in your life could turn into strongholds of sin? How will you fight this sin?

Victory in Jesus!

If a big dog and a small dog get into a fight, which usually wins? Usually the big dog wins. Little dogs just aren't strong enough to win over bigger, stronger dogs. Do you know what little dogs often do when they are confronted by bigger dogs? They *act* like they are ferocious. They bark, run around, and bare their teeth. They try to scare big dogs by acting like they are more ferocious than they really are. They pretend to be strong and fierce, but they aren't.

Satan is a lot like the little dog pretending to be greater and stronger than he really is. Jesus is greater than Satan. He is more powerful and smarter. When Jesus died on the cross, He took the punishment for man's sin and made a way for us to be right with God. That was very bad news for God's enemy, Satan.

> The reason the Son of God appeared was to destroy the works of the devil. (1 John 3:8)

That means that Satan is a defeated enemy! Everyone who trusts in Jesus has His power to fight against the work of Satan. Jesus has already won the fight of faith for His children. Christians are winners because Jesus is the winner! Christians have victory because Jesus is victorious!

> But thanks be to God, who gives us the victory through our Lord Jesus Christ. (1 Corinthians 15:57)

Do you remember that Peter said he would never fall away from Jesus? He said he would even die for Jesus. What did he and the other disciples do when the crowd came to arrest Jesus? They all left Jesus and ran away!

But after Jesus died on the cross and rose again, He promised to send the Holy Spirit, who would make His people strong. And it happened just like Jesus said. After Jesus sent the Holy Spirit, Peter was able to fight the fight of faith with great strength.

One day Peter and John were going to the temple when a lame man—a man who couldn't walk—asked for money. Peter told the lame man that he didn't have any money but offered him something much better. He looked at the lame man and said, "In the name of Jesus . . . rise up and walk!" (Acts 3:6). Not only did the lame man get up and walk, he was leaping and praising God!

The crowd of people there were amazed. Peter told them that the lame man was healed by the power of Jesus. Then he told them who Jesus was and that He died for their sins. Instead of turning to Jesus, the rulers were upset that the disciples were preaching about Jesus, and they put Peter and John in prison.

But this time Peter did not deny Jesus. When he was questioned, he boldly told the rulers about Jesus. Even when Peter and John were told never to preach about Jesus again, they bravely said they could not stop speaking about Jesus. They stood strong in the power of Jesus and were victorious. They were winners in the fight of faith!

If you are a Christian, you have the power of Jesus in you. He will help you to fight the fight of faith. But Satan, like a little dog, acts fierce and tries to make us think he is more powerful than he really is. He tries to make us forget that we have victory in Jesus. He tries to make us think and feel things like, "I can't fight this spirit of fear. I am going to be fearful all my life." But that is a lie from Satan, who is the Father of Lies. Jesus defeated the works of Satan, and Jesus defeated Satan—and Jesus is in us if we are His children.

When a thought comes into our heads, we should "capture" it—hold it and bring it to Jesus. Say, "Jesus, is this true? Is it true that I cannot defeat a spirit of fear?" Or bring that thought to the Word of God: "Is this what the Bible teaches?" The Bible teaches that Jesus destroyed the Devil's work. Because the spirit of fear is the work of Satan, we do not have to accept it. It is a destroyed work. God "gives us the victory through our Lord Jesus Christ." When we capture the thought that we cannot defeat a spirit of fear and bring it to Jesus and the Word of God, we see that it is a lie.

We destroy arguments and every lofty opinion raised against the knowledge of God, and take every thought captive to obey Christ. (2 Corinthians 10:5)

Victory belongs to the Christian. But if we forget that Jesus in us is stronger than Satan, we will not live in victory. We will listen to Satan's lies and be fooled by his deception. Our attitude toward Satan should be, "Leave me alone! You are full of lies! I will not listen to your lies. You are a defeated enemy. Jesus in me is stronger than you are. Get lost!" Then we will walk in victory.

Little children, you are from God and have overcome them, for he who is in you is greater than he who is in the world. (1 John 4:4)

LEARNING TO TRUST GOD

✤ Read about the victory that Peter and John had through Jesus in Acts 4:5–22. What spiritual battles did Peter and John fight? How did they have the power to fight these battles?

✤ Read 1 John 4:1–6. What does "overcome" mean? Who is "he who is in you" and "he who is in the world"? How is Satan like the little dog? What does he do to intimidate (frighten) us? Pray that you will trust Jesus and that He will give you victory.

✤ *Activity:* Make up a cheer proclaiming the Christian's victory in Jesus.

Aliens and Strangers

Have you ever watched a race? During the race, did the winner look around, stop to tie his shoe, take a break, stop and talk with people, and pet a dog? What did he do?

To win a race, a person has to concentrate, work hard, and keep running. He can't quit, and he can't dawdle. He has to throw his whole self into winning and head for the goal with energy. This is what it takes to win.

This is also what it takes to win the fight of faith. It takes not giving up, but standing strong with the help of God. Winners don't give up. They keep going even when it is hard.

God has been so good to give us examples of people who stood strong—people like Abel, Noah, Abraham, Sarah, Isaac, Jacob, Joseph, Moses, Gideon, David, Samuel, and others. Hebrews 11 tells us that they were badly treated, mocked, beaten, put in prison, stoned, and even killed.[1] But they did not give up. They held onto their faith. They did not stop trusting in God.

How could they fight the fight of faith without giving up?

All these people were still living by faith when they died. . . . And they admitted that they were aliens and strangers on earth. People who say such things show that they are looking for a country of their own . . . they were longing for a better country—a heavenly one. Therefore God is not ashamed to be called their God, for he has prepared a city for them. (Hebrews 11:13–14, 16 NIV)

They didn't give up because they knew they were "strangers and aliens on the earth." Do you know what an alien is? An alien is someone from another country.

1. See Hebrews 11:32–38.

The men and women who held on in faith and did not give up understood that this world was not their home. They were here for just a while, so it didn't matter so much what happened here. They knew that their real, forever home is heaven. They knew that winning the fight of faith would mean living in heaven forever. And this is what they knew about heaven:

> And I heard a loud voice from the throne saying, "Behold, the dwelling place of God is with man. He will dwell with them, and they will be his people, and God himself will be with them as their God. He will wipe away

every tear from their eyes, and death shall be no more, neither shall there be mourning, nor crying, nor pain anymore, for the former things have passed away." . . .

The one who conquers will have this heritage, and I will be his God and he will be my son. (Revelation 21:3–4, 7)

And night will be no more. They will need no light of lamp or sun, for the Lord God will be their light, and they will reign forever and ever. (Revelation 22:5)

What a wonderful place heaven is! This was the better place that the Hebrews 11 people were longing for. Heaven was their real home, and they kept thinking about it. They couldn't wait to get there.

If you are a child of God, eternity in heaven with God is where you really belong. The way you hang onto your faith is to think about heaven—the eternal place that Jesus is preparing for you. Just think about what is waiting for you in heaven as a child of God. There will be no tears or death or pain, and no darkness. You will be with Jesus, and you will rule with Him forever. Why would you ever give up in the fight of faith and risk losing heaven?

Have you ever seen someone from another country? Did he look, dress, talk, and think like you? People from other countries are different from you. This is the way Christians should look to people who are not Christians. We are not supposed to "fit in." We are not supposed to talk like non-Christians or think like them, because we are not part of this world. Christians talk about God and heaven. We believe things are wrong that others don't think are wrong. Non-Christians will be interested in things that don't interest us. Our faith will be important to us, but not to them. It is okay that we are not like the world; we are supposed to be different. We are aliens and strangers here. If you are a Christian, this world is not your home. So if people make fun of us for believing in Jesus, it does not matter. They cannot understand, because they are from a different world than we are.

Fighting the fight of faith is like a running a race. We must set our eyes on the goal of eternal life in heaven with Jesus. We cannot give up until we get to the finish line at death.

> But one thing I do: forgetting what lies behind and straining forward to what lies ahead, I press on toward the goal for the prize of the upward call of God in Christ Jesus. (Philippians 3:13–14)

The way to win the fight of faith is to forget about the unimportant things in this world and "strain forward." We persevere in faith by thinking about the joys of heaven.

If you are not trusting in Jesus, put your trust in Him today! Ask Him to give you a new heart of faith and to help you stand firm in faith until He takes you home to heaven. On that day you will be able to say,

> I have fought the good fight, I have finished the race, I have kept the faith. (2 Timothy 4:7)

LEARNING TO TRUST GOD

✛ Read Revelation 21:1–8. What is heaven like? What will happen to those who are not trusting in Jesus? Ask Jesus to give you faith in Him.

✛ Read Philippians 3:13–14. What "lies behind"? What "lies ahead"? What is the prize? What does the word "straining" show you? How is fighting the fight of faith our work and God's work?

✛ *Activity:* Watch a race. How is this similar to fighting the fight of faith? Write some postcards encouraging others to trust in Jesus and persevere in faith. Before putting them in the mail, pray for those receiving the cards.

A Final Thought: Just Keep Stepping[1]

Have you ever run in a race? How long was it?

In 1928, the International Transcontinental Foot Race (nicknamed the Bunion Derby) was announced. The prize money was $25,000, and the race was from Los Angeles, California, to New York City! How could anyone run that far?

There were 199 people in the race, including twenty-year-old Andy Payne. Andy was a Cherokee Indian from Oklahoma, the oldest of seven children. He wanted the prize money to pay off what was owed on the family farm.

The runners, from 24 different countries, lined up at the starting line on March 4, 1928, and set out for New York. By the end of the first week, 70 runners had dropped out. But Andy kept running. He ran in the rain, in snow, and on hot sunny days. He ran on gravel roads through the desert and uphill through the mountains. Day after day he kept running. His motto—what he kept saying to himself—was "Just keep stepping from day to day."

On May 26, Andy crossed the finish line first and won the prize. He ran 3,421.5 miles in 84 days. He just kept stepping from day to day to finish the race.

If you are a Christian, you are running a much more important race—the race of faith. There will be hard days in the race—days when you feel like giving up. But "just keep stepping from day to day" until you cross the finish line and receive your heavenly reward.

It is easy to start a race. But it is much harder to finish it. To finish, you cannot give up. You must keep running, even when running is hard to do. Ask Jesus to help you finish your race of faith and "just keep stepping from day to day."

1. The facts in this story are taken from an article by Veda Boyd Jones titled "The Winner of the Bunion Derby," published in the *Harris' Farmer's Almanac*.

Scripture Memory

The life of faith is a fight of faith, and believers must be armed for this fight. This fight is not against flesh and blood, but against spiritual principalities, so the Word of God is our indispensable sword. Through our memorizing and meditating on the Word, this powerful sword becomes readily available to us at any time, providing us with ever-present counsel, encouragement, and protection from the enemy of our souls. Children Desiring God offers a variety of tools for preschoolers through adults. We pray that God would instill your heart with the conviction and yearning to memorize His Word so that it becomes a lifelong practice.

Fighter Verses

The Fighter Verses focus on the character and worth of our great God, encourage believers to battle against our fleshly desires, and remind believers of the hope of the gospel. This five-year memory program is a revision of the original Legacy Verses and contains most of the original verses as well as some new ones. It is available in a two-ring binder with five sets of yearly verses.

The Fighter Verse App

The Fighter Verse App is now available for iPhone® and iPad®, Android®, and Kindle®. The App was created as a tool to help encourage Bible memory.

Fighter Verse Songs

Every Fighter Verse™ Song CD includes word-for-word Bible passages (English Standard Version) set to music. These passages are specifically selected to help believers fight the fight of faith.

Fighter Verses—Extended

The Extended Memory Set is designed for those wishing to memorize longer passages of Scripture. Still structured as a five-year program, this set will walk you through memorizing large segments or whole New Testament epistles, the Sermon on the Mount, etc.

Foundation Verses

Foundation Verses are strategically chosen Bible verses for children in preschool through age five. The pack includes verses designed to lay a firm scriptural foundation of basic biblical truth that will pave the way for a faith response.

More resources are available at FighterVerses.com, including free Bible memory helps and review tools, a weekly blog, downloadable resources, songs, audio, links to Bible memory encouragement from the ministry of John Piper, and much more.

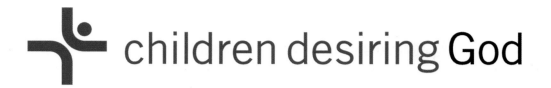

children desiring God

This storybook was adapted from *Fight the Good Fight*, an upper-elementary Sunday school curriculum published by Children Desiring God (CDG). If you would like to further explore persevering in faith with your child, resources are available from Children Desiring God.

Children Desiring God is a nonprofit ministry that Sally Michael and her husband, David Michael, helped to establish in the late 1990s. CDG publishes God-centered, Bible-saturated, Christ-exalting resources to help parents and churches train their children spiritually in the hope that the next generation will see and embrace Jesus Christ as the one who saves and satisfies the soul. Resources include curriculum for children of nursery age through youth (see sequence chart on following page), parenting booklets, and Bible memory resources. Free parenting and Christian education training audio and video resources are also available online.

Please contact us if we can partner with you for the joy of the next generation.

childrendesiringGOD.org
info@childrendesiringGOD.org

SUNDAY SCHOOL	
Nursery	**A Sure Foundation** A Philosophy and Curriculum for Ministry to Infants and Toddlers
Preschool	**He Established a Testimony** Old Testament Stories for Young Children
Preschool	**He Has Spoken By His Son** New Testament Stories for Young Children

	SUNDAY SCHOOL	MIDWEEK
K	**Jesus, What a Savior!** A Study for Children on Redemption	**He Has Been Clearly Seen** A Study for Children on Seeing and Delighting in God's Glory
1	**The ABCs of God** A Study for Children on the Greatness and Worth of God	**I Stand in Awe** A Study for Children on the Bible
2	**Faithful to All His Promises** A Study for Children on the Promises of God	(Children Desiring God will announce plans for this title in the future.)
3	**In the Beginning . . . Jesus** A Chronological Study for Children on Redemptive History	**The Way of the Wise** A Study for Children on Wisdom and Foolishness
4	**To Be Like Jesus** A Study for Children on Following Jesus	**I Will Build My Church** A Study for Children on the Church (future release)
5	**How Majestic Is Your Name** A Study for Children on the Names and Character of God	**Fight the Good Fight** A Study for Children on Persevering in Faith
6	**My Purpose Will Stand** A Study for Children on the Providence of God	**Pour Out Your Heart Before Him** A Study for Children on Prayer and Praise in the Psalms (future release)
7	**Your Word Is Truth** A Study for Youth on Seeing All of Life through the Truth of Scripture	**Abiding in Jesus** A Study for Youth on Trusting Jesus and Encouraging Others
8	**Teach Me Your Way** A Study for Youth on Surrender to Jesus and Submission to His Way	**Rejoicing in God's Good Design** A Study for Youth on Biblical Manhood and Womanhood

Also by Sally Michael

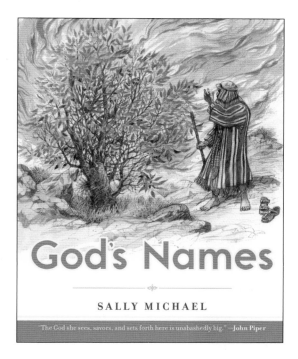

When you want to get to know someone, where do you start? How do you introduce yourself?

Usually you start with someone's name.

God knows this—and he doesn't have just one name to share with us, either! The Bible gives us many names for God and tells us what they all mean. And when we learn a new name for God, we learn something new about him, too!

This book is for you and your children to read together. Every chapter teaches something new and helps put you—and your children—on the right track in your relationship with God.

God has left his names with his people so they can know him . . . and through these pages your children can know him too.

"The God she sees, savors, and sets forth here is unabashedly big. Not distant and uncaring. But great enough to make his caring count."
—JOHN PIPER, Pastor for Preaching and Vision, Bethlehem Baptist Church, Minneapolis, MN

"Sally Michael creatively helps parents to lead their children through a fun and fascinating exploration of the various ways God's names reveal the beauty and power of his character and actions."
—JUSTIN TAYLOR, Managing Editor, *ESV Study Bible*

"Grandparents and parents and all the extended family, as well as those who make up the church of the living God—all have a divine unction to pass along God's truth to the hearts of our children! Sally Michael has given us an excellent tool in *God's Names* to do just that!"
—DOROTHY PATTERSON, General Editor of *The Woman's Study Bible* and Professor of Theology in Woman's Studies, Southwestern Baptist Theological Seminary

Also by Sally Michael

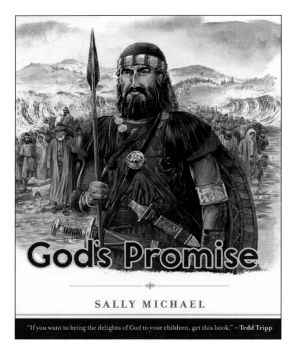

This book, for you and your children to read together, will help them learn these promises and put their own confidence in them. Each chapter looks at a new promise and explores it in the context of a Bible story.

God has left his promises with his people so they can trust him . . . and through these pages your children can trust him too.

You have probably seen your children's eyes light up at receiving a present.

How excited would they be to get a present directly from God?

God already has a present to offer your children. And you can be the one who helps them discover it.

God has left all of his children many promises through his Word as gifts that flow from his goodness and love. Each one is backed up by his power and trustworthy character, so we can be confident in them.

"This engaging, attractively illustrated book teaches not only the promises of the Bible, but also the character of the God who makes and keeps his promises."
—TEDD TRIPP, President of Shepherding the Heart Ministries

"This book is clear, profound, helpful, and at every point grounded with faith and confidence in who God is. A tremendous resource!"
—ELIZABETH GROVES, Lecturer in Old Testament, Westminster Seminary

"Sally Michael does not sugarcoat any of the more difficult promises, but explains them in a way that shows a high view of God. . . . I highly recommend it."
—MARTHA PEACE, Biblical Counselor, Co-author of *The Faithful Parent*

Also by Sally Michael

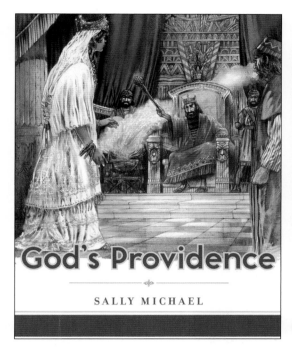

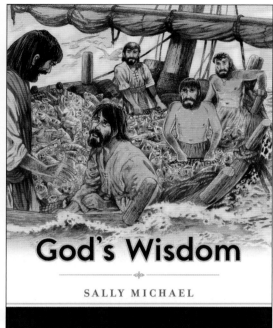

Sally Michael believes that a child who can embrace God's providence can rest in God's sovereign care, and she uses simple truths to help you explain God's providence to all your children. She moves on to show children how God's providence applies to all of life and creation . . . including themselves.

"My heart soars with worship and joy and zeal as I page through Sally's new book, *God's Providence*. . . . Here is a foundation for life that is solid enough to sustain parents and children through the hardest times they will ever face. . . . And here is practical application for children and those who love them enough to teach them."
—JOHN PIPER, Author; Associate Pastor for Preaching and Vision, Chancellor, Bethlehem College and Seminary

Through these teachings and stories from the Bible, Sally Michael describes for parents and children the characteristics of the foolish and the wise, contrasts for them the way of wisdom with the way of foolishness, and shows them the end result of each path. Explore these two paths with your own child, and let the words of Proverbs encourage them on the life-giving path of wisdom.

"Sally Michael seamlessly weaves New Testament and Old Testament stories together to teach biblical wisdom in a way that is clear, fun, and engaging for children. Her compelling word pictures and analogies make difficult concepts easier to grasp."
—MARTY MACHOWSKI, Pastor, Author of *Long Story Short* and *The Gospel Story Bible*

Also by Sally Michael

Our children are special to us, and Christmas is a special time for *them*, captivating them with its joy and wonder.

What better time for parents to introduce their young children to the most special child ever born— the child who is also the Savior of the world and the King of all Kings?

Sally Michael helps parents to share the story of the birth of Jesus with their children and goes a step further by placing the Christmas story in the larger context of the Bible—what comes before and after. She motivates even the youngest children to teach this all-important story to others after they have learned it for themselves.

Through its large, full-color illustrated pages and its suggestions for accompanying songs and visuals, this book will help children to learn by heart the most special story ever told.

"The simplicity of this book mirrors the plainness of the biblical story. Carol lyrics waft beside the brief, deep Scriptures that inspired them. In these pages the Savior is clearly worshiped—the story of his arrival touched me yet again."
—STEVE ESTES, Author of *A Better December*